Presented to

_____

By

_____

On the Occasion of

_____

Date

_____

FLOWERS ALONG *the* PATH

*Collected Wisdom for
Your Spiritual Journey*

ESTHER CARLS DODGEN

BARBOUR
PUBLISHING, INC.
Uhrichsville, Ohio

Published by Barbour Publishing, Inc., P.O. Box 719, Uhrichsville, Ohio 44683 http://www.barbourbooks.com

 Member of the
Evangelical Christian
Publishers Association

Printed in the United States of America.

PREFACE

God has appeared in my life in so many extraordinary ways, but mainly through the people who have touched my life and inspired me along my life's journey. My family, especially my husband and best friend Joe; my close friends; and my extended spiritual family have all been God's instruments in bringing me to this moment in time and to this stage in my spiritual development.

As I look back, I can see how God has brought people into my life at crucial times—people like my first-year college professor, Glenda, who was an inspiration to me; my dear friend and spiritual mentor, Vera, who appeared at the beginning of my teaching career when I ventured out all alone; my teaching colleague, Mary, who challenged and encouraged me in my faith and writing abilities; and my sister and true friend, Ruth, who has been there all along. I owe a special thanks to my literary advisors and supporters: Glen, Dave, Betty, Ruth, Lois, Dale, Mary, Jim, David, Helen, James, Barbara, and especially Susan and Paul of Barbour Publishing, who were of immense help in finalizing the manuscript.

When I started this project I did not know what form it would take or what purpose it would serve, but I knew I had to proceed. The call was as clear as the ringing of a bell on a clear, crisp morning. Being given the opportunity to compile this anthology has truly been a gift from God. I have deeply sensed His abiding presence and guidance while working on it.

The assignment has been completed. Now I dedicate it to all those who seek the cultivation of the combined inner (spiritual) and outer (service-oriented) dimensions of their lives. My fervent prayer is that anyone who reads any portion of this collected wisdom will find clues to the path that leads home and will receive encouragement and inspiration to seek God further. May our lives be enriched by gathering a few of these spiritual flowers and sharing them with others as we journey together in His name.

Contents

PART SIX
THE GIVING SOUL—
THE OUTWARD JOURNEY,
EXPANDING IN GROWTH TO
INCLUDE OTHERS

INTRODUCTION

I quote others only the better to understand myself.

MICHEL DE MONTAIGNE

This anthology of spiritual writings can be compared to a flower garden sown with inspirational seeds gathered from many lands, from many ages, and from a great company of God's disciples from all walks of life. These seeds have been arranged, grouped, and planted in an order following my personal spiritual journey from darkness to light and, subsequently, my attempts to grow in that light. They have sprouted, taken root, bloomed, and become my own garden of inspiration. The flowers produced are of a personal and inspirational nature. Included in the anthology are selections of nonfictional prose and poetry from a wide range of writers in whose ideas I have found a sense of real worth and a parallel to my own spiritual pilgrimage.

This experiential endeavor is an attempt to clarify my own journey toward God and to explore the formative influences of this journey. Thus what I offer in these pages are simply glimpses into my searching as a fellow pilgrim. This inner journey has to do with loving God and attempting to live in such a way that one's whole life somehow depends on being faithful to Him. This compilation is also an effort to capture the essence of all basic spiritual truth. Whether the compiler has accomplished that will be for the reader to determine. It will appeal to anyone interested in spiritual matters, including Christian readers of all denominations as well as non-churchgoers who are seeking answers to spiritual questions.

As we walk together on this inward pilgrimage and are illuminated by some of the great spiritual classics, it is my hope you will find a vivid sense of an encompassing fellowship of those, from all the Christian ages, who have experienced the joy of knowing God. May we realize God's will for us to be one with Him and enter more deeply into that fellowship. The riches of all are ours to share and enjoy. Let us light the flame of our minds from these words and draw from the refreshing waters of spiritual truth of these pages to help bring to fulfillment the desire for Him that He has placed within us and to learn those lessons of the abundant life that Christ so eloquently taught.

Spiritual reading is, or at least can be,
second only to prayer as a developer
and supporter of the inner life.

EVELYN UNDERHILL

God be thanked for books;
they are the voices of the distant and the dead,
and make us heirs of the spiritual life of past ages.

WILLIAM ELLERY CHANNING

The constant habit of perusing devout books
is so indispensable,
that it has been termed oil for the lamp of prayer.

HANNAH MORE

Whatever we may say against collections,
which present authors in a disjointed form,
they nevertheless bring about many excellent results.
We are not always so composed,
so full of wisdom, that we are able to take in at once
the whole scope of a work
according to its merits.

JOHANN WOLFGANG VON GOETHE

Read not to contradict and confute,
nor to believe and take for granted,
nor to find talk and discourse,
but to weigh and consider.

FRANCIS BACON

A word aptly spoken is like apples of gold
in settings of silver.

PROVERBS 25:11

PART ONE

THE SEEKING SOUL—
IN QUEST OF THE PEARL
OF GREAT PRICE

Begin to search and dig in your own field for this
pearl of eternity that lies hidden in it;
it cannot cost you too much,
nor can you buy it too dear, for it is all;
and when you have found it,
you will know that all which you have sold
or given away for it is as mere a nothing,
as a bubble upon the water.

WILLIAM LAW

CHAPTER 1

GOD SEEKS US OUT
AND CALLS US TO HIM

Whether you turn to the right or to the left,
your ears will hear a voice behind you, saying,
"This is the way; walk in it."

ISAIAH 30:21

God made us in order to have fellowship with Him. He is continually seeking us out and calling us to awaken to the joy of loving and being loved by Him. How can we awaken to His call if we have been asleep? Every awakening to God begins with a knock, a still small voice speaking, bearing "witness with our spirits that we are children of God." It is as clear as the ringing of a bell in the quiet of the evening. We have been hearing this knock as far back as we can remember. He has been saying, "You are on the wrong track. Turn around. I am here. I am the Way, the Truth, and the Life." If we really hear Him in the depths of our heart, we will recognize this tug of the Holy Spirit upon our heart and know that God is there.

GOD PUTS THE LONGING
FOR HIM IN OUR HEARTS

God created humanity for
a love relationship with Him.
More than anything else,
God wants us to love Him with our total being.
He is the One who initiates the love relationship.

HENRY T. BLACKABY AND CLAUDE V. KING
Experiencing God

Here I am! I stand at the door and knock.
If anyone hears my voice
and opens the door,
I will come in and eat with him,
and he with me.

REVELATION 3:20

God formed us for His pleasure,
and so formed us that we, as well as He,
can, in divine communion,
enjoy the sweet and mysterious mingling
of kindred personalities.
He meant us to seek Him and live with Him
and draw our life from His smile.

A.W. TOZER
The Pursuit of God

The soul of man bears the image of God;
so nothing can satisfy it but
He whose image it bears.
Our soul, says Augustine,
was created as by God, so for God,
and is therefore never quiet
till it rest in God.

THOMAS GATAKER

To seek God means first of all to
let yourself be found by Him.

BRAKKENSTEIN COMMUNITY

If we are completely honest with ourselves we know deep down in our hearts that the usual goals and strivings of self-sufficiency and self-fulfillment we have are not our real destiny. We sense an uneasiness with the common, ordinary life of delights and pleasures, and begin to hear this quiet voice from the soul's depths, a whispering of a more meaningful, richer life. We are in essence seeking God and feel that He is indeed drawing us to Him. When we respond, it is to God that we are responding.

CLARA M. MATHESON (C. M. M.)

The Son of Man came to seek and to save what was lost."
LUKE 19:10

While you are seeking you are also being sought. You will not be lost, you will not miss the gate. God will find you and lead you. You will find God revealing Himself all around you. Look and you will find Him. Bells will ring and gongs will resound. Choruses will sing and trumpets will blare, calling us to a grander view. A voice within our soul will whisper to us that there is more to life

than these goals and securities for which we strive.
We will know that we are being led.

C. M. M.

I fled Him, down the nights and down the days;
I fled Him down the arches of the years;
I fled Him, down the labyrinthine ways
Of my own mind; and in the midst of tears
I hid from Him, and under running laughter
Up vistaed hopes, I sped;
And shot, precipitated,
Adown Titanic gloom of chasmed fears
From those strong Feet that followed, followed after.

Francis Thompson
from *The Hound of Heaven*

In looking over my past experience, I cannot resist
the conviction that it has not been primarily my
seeking and searching that has been important,
but rather the awareness of being sought and
found by Another. . . . It is He who "fashions" and
"creates" and "finds," and thus gives existence. It is
He who "speaks" and reveals His will, and sets life
before its imperative.

John Mullenberg

*I led them with cords of human kindness,
with ties of love."*

Hosea 11:4

Gold, even though you desire it,
you may perhaps never possess;
God you will possess as soon as you desire Him.
For He came to you before you desired Him;
when your will was turned away from Him
He called you.

Augustine of Hippo

*No one can come to me unless
the Father who sent me draws him,
and I will raise him up at the last day."*

John 6:44

We do not always need
to seek God in the Bible,
for in the Bible God is seeking us,
and He will surely find us,
if we are ready to be found of Him.

WASHINGTON GLADDEN
The Christian Way

Fear not, for I have redeemed you;
I have summoned you by name; you are mine."

ISAIAH 43:1

What, dear brothers,
is more delightful than
this voice of the Lord calling to us?
See how the Lord in His love
shows us the way of life.

from PROLOGUE OF THE RULE OF ST. BENEDICT

Who answers Christ's insistent call
Must give himself, his life, his all,
Without one backward look.
Who sets his hand unto the plow,
And glances back with anxious brow.
His calling hath mistook.
Christ claims him wholly for His own:
He must be Christ's and Christ's alone.

John Oxenham
from *Follow Me*

The true life has been given to men, and men know it. They hear its summons, but, always swept on by the cares of the moment, they are withheld from it. The true life is as though a rich man gave a feast, and summoned the guests, His call to them in the voice of the Spirit of the Father inviting all men to Himself. But of those invited some are busy in commerce, some in the household, some in family affairs—none come to the feast. Only the poor, such as have no cares of the body, come to the feast, and gain happiness. So men, distracting themselves with cares for the bodily life, are losing the true life. He who cannot, and that altogether, decline the cares and gains of the bodily life, cannot fulfill the

Father's will, because one cannot serve oneself a little, and the Father a little.   LEO TOLSTOY
The Collected Works of Leo Tolstoy

Live lives worthy of God,
who calls you into his kingdom and glory.

1 THESSALONIANS 2:12

*God often visits us but most of the time
we are not at home.*

JOSEPH ROUX
Meditations of a Parish Priest

In the midst of all the sounds rising above all the mingled words there is a strange Voice—but not quite a stranger. A man recognizes it. It seems to come from every part of him but cannot rest itself on any point of sound. He waits. He listens. When all is still, he listens now at a deeper level of silence. In soundless movement there floats up through all the chambers of his being, encompassing all the tongued cries from many selves, one word: God—

God—God. And the answer is the same, filling all the living silence before Thy Face: God—God—God.

HOWARD THURMAN
The Inward Journey

The LORD *appeared to us in the past, saying:*
"I have loved you
with an everlasting love;
I have drawn you with loving-kindness."

JEREMIAH 31:3

CLOSING PRAYER

Lord Jesus Christ,
thank You for giving us the power to seek
You and in seeking to find You.
You want us to know You and turn to You.
Lord, I hear Your call and will follow.
Amen.

CHAPTER 2

EVERYONE HAS
AN INNATE NEED FOR GOD

He satisfies the thirsty and
fills the hungry with good things.

PSALM 107:9

Fellowship with God is the deepest joy of human existence. He is our soul's necessity, its deepest hunger. Our need for fulfillment is in reality an expression of our hunger and thirst for God. God afflicts us with this feeling of uselessness so we will seek Him. We are searching for a kind of unity in the diverse experiences of life, a key to unlock the secret of meaning and purpose in life. We are consciously drawn to Him as the only answer to our yearning. God is sowing the first seeds of faith in our souls. There is nothing—no possession or person who can give us meaning in our lives. We were not meant for a life without God and we cannot be satisfied with anything less than this fellowship with Him. Even though we are unaware of the countless times He draws near, speaking to deaf ears, appearing to blind eyes because we are so preoccupied with our own busy cares, there will come a time when we will realize our utter futility without God and will awaken from our slumber and see our need for God.

Our Deepest Need Is for God

The knowledge of God is naturally implanted in all.

Thomas Aquinas
Summa Theologica

The deepest need of man is not food and clothing and shelter, important as they are. It is God. We have mistaken the nature of poverty, and thought it was economic poverty. No, it is poverty of soul, deprivation of God's recreating, loving peace.

Thomas R. Kelly
A Testament of Devotion

God dwells in a secret and hidden way in all souls,
in their very substance,
for if He did not,
they could not exist at all.

JOHN OF THE CROSS

Let a man try to live with no sky, no God in his thoughts, no aspiration, nor adoration, nor awe of soul; let him throw the reins on the back of his body, and let the senses do as they please; let him live for himself alone and stay unmoved in bed with his children when his neighbor lacks bread, or warm in his purple and luxuriating at his feast when Lazarus lies cold and hungry at his gate, and is there any one who will doubt, long before the end of things, that that is not what a man is for?

MALTBIE D. BABCOCK
Thoughts for Every-Day Living

The soul awaits in wonder
and works in reverence
for what God shall reveal to her.

PLATO

No one will know much about the experience of the spirit until he has faced his need to know. "Blessed are the hungry," said Jesus. . . . Some have been awakened to their need to know and others have not.

Ralph S. Cushman
Spiritual Hilltops

If a man is not made for God,
why is he happy only in God?
If man is made for God,
why is he opposed to God?

Blaise Pascal
Pensees

An immortal soul, from its very nature, cannot find what it needs anywhere except in God Himself. True religion begins in the heart. It is not a mere set of rules to be obeyed—an example to be copied. It is Christ coming into the heart and dwelling there.

James R. Miller

We have all of us free access to all that is great, and good, and happy, and carry within ourselves a key to all the treasures that heaven has to bestow upon us. We starve in the midst of plenty, groan under infirmities, with the remedy in our own hand; live and die without knowing and feeling anything of the One only God, whilst we have it in our power to know and enjoy it in as great a reality as we know and feel the power of this world over us; for Heaven is as near to our souls as this world is to our bodies; and we are created, we are redeemed, to have our conversation in it.

WILLIAM LAW
The Spirit of Prayer

*How ever far back we go
in the history of the race,
we can never find a time or place
where man was not conscious of the soul
and of a divine power on which
his life depended.*

CHRISTOPHER DAWSON
Religion and Culture

I don't care what they say with their mouths—everybody knows that something is eternal. And it ain't houses, and it ain't names, and it ain't earth, and it ain't even stars—everybody knows in their bones that something has to do with human beings. All the greatest people ever lived have been telling us that for five thousand years and yet you'd be surprised how people are always losing hold of it. There's something way down deep that's eternal about every human being.

THORNTON WILDER
Our Town

He is the great answer to loneliness. Without Him, we shall always be lonely, no matter what human friends we have. There is none other with whom we can be perfectly frank; none other to whom we can tell all our sins and sorrows; none other with whom we can share all our hopes and dreams. Only God has the capacity to understand everything—to forgive everything—to make allowance for every error—to know why we did what we did—why we want what we want—why we fear what we fear—why we hope what we hope. Only God can understand in us all that we cannot understand in ourselves. God is the only one who in

Himself can satisfy ourselves. God Himself, not what He can do for us, but what He is, is the answer—as water to thirst, as food to hunger, as truth to a puzzled mind, as beauty to the artist.

ALBERT E. DAY
An Autobiography of Prayer

Our souls were made to
"mount up with wings,"
and they can never be satisfied with
anything short of flying.
Our souls chafe and fret,
and cry out for freedom.

HANNAH WHITALL SMITH
The Christian's Secret of a Happy Life

In each heart there is a secret garden which God made uniquely for Himself.

FULTON J. SHEEN

Truth is within ourselves; it takes no rise
From outward things, whate'er you may believe.
There is an inmost center in us all,
Where truth abides in fullness; and around,
Wall upon wall, the gross flesh hems it in,
A baffling and perverting carnal mesh
Binds it, and makes all error; and, to know
Rather consists in opening out a way
Whence the imprisoned splendor may escape
Than in effecting entry for a light
Supposed to be without.

ROBERT BROWNING
from *Paracelsus*

The wonder is not that there should be obstacles and sufferings in this world, but that there should be law and order, beauty and joy, goodness and love. The idea of God that man has in his being is the wonder of all wonders. He has felt in the depths of his life that what appears as imperfect is the manifestation of the perfect; just as a man who has an ear for music realizes the perfection of a song, while in fact he is only listening to a succession of notes.

VICTOR GOLLANCZ
Man and God

The spiritual life is not a special career, involving abstraction from the world of things. It is a part of every man's life; and until he has realized it he is not a complete human being, has not entered into possession of all his powers.

EVELYN UNDERHILL
Practical Mysticism

There is a God-shaped vacuum in every heart.

BLAISE PASCAL
Pensees

Thou hast made us for Thyself," cries St. Augustine, "and our heart finds no rest until it reposes in Thee." This truth is the first principle of all morality; reason, religion and experience all unite in proving it to us.

JEAN-NICOLAS GROU
Manual for Interior Souls

There is but one thing needful—to possess God.
All our senses, all our powers of mind and soul. . .
are so many ways of approaching the divinity, so
many modes of tasting and adoring God.

HENRI-FREDERIC AMIEL
Journal

Men are children of this world,
Yet hath God set eternity in their hearts
As a firm possession,
    from the day that He created them.

The world is like a flowing brook,
They drink of it and are not sated,
They would not be satisfied
Were the sea emptied therein.

It is as though the water were strong brine,
And the craving of their hearts
    impelled them to drink thereof—
Like a torrent would it rush into their throats,
But their thirst would remain unquenched forever.

ABRAHAM BEN MEIR IBN-EZRA

Man needs Jesus Christ as a necessity and not as a luxury. You may be pleased to have flowers, but you must have bread. . . . Jesus is not a phenomenon, He is bread: Christ is not a curiosity, He is water. As surely as we cannot live without bread, we cannot live truly without Christ: If we know not Christ we are not living, our movement is a mechanical flutter, our pulse is but the stirring of an animal life.   JOSEPH PARKER

With partridges, it often occurs that some steal the eggs of others, in order to brood, and it is a strange but nevertheless well-attested fact that when the chick, hatched and nourished under the wing of the thievish partridge, first hears the cry of its true mother, it forthwith quits its thievish partridge, and hurries to meet and follow its own parent, drawn by its correspondence with her, which had remained hidden and as though sleeping in the depth of its nature, until the encounter of each with each.

Thus it is with our heart, for although hatched, nourished, and brought up among the temporal, low, and transitory, yet at the first look it casts toward God, at the first consciousness inspired by Him, the natural inborn inclination to love Him, slumbering and imperceptible till now, awakes in an instant unawares, as a spark among ashes, and affecting the will, gives it an impulse of the supreme love due to the Sovereign and First Principle of all things.

FRANCIS DE SALES
Spiritual Conferences

Who can resist the conclusion
that under the matter must be
something superior which our languages,
doing the best they can, call spirit?

ERNEST DIMNET
What We Live By

*What frightens me is that men are
content with what is not life at all.*

ELIZABETH BARRETT BROWNING

Who except God can give you Peace?
Has the world ever been able to satisfy the heart?

GERARD MAJELLA

God is, and all is well.

JOHN GREENLEAF WHITTIER,
from "My Birthday"

We have all kinds of alibis to hide behind that keep us distracted from the truth. As we watch people in their struggle to always be in human company, to escape from solitude and thoughts of the eternal, all the time seeking distractions from themselves, let us allow God's Spirit in us go out to them and realize how much all people need God and how much God loves them. We know they cannot keep going on like that. One day they will realize the dead-end street they are on and they will stop. They will not be able to run any more. They will become sick of their frenzied activity and all their hiding places. They will finally realize that God is there in the silence of their hearts and He has been there all the time. They simply will become quiet enough to hear His gentle invitation to "Come." They then will acknowledge Him and become children of God.

C. M. M.

CLOSING PRAYER

Lord Jesus, help us to realize that we need You.
It is so easy to get distracted by
the events and people around us.
We bow down now in humble acknowledgment
of Your life-giving power.
Make us into Your servants now,
we pray in Jesus' name. Amen.

CHAPTER 3

How to Find God

*Come near to God
and he will come near to you.*

JAMES 4:8

Jesus came to show the way to an abundant life, a way to think, a way to act, a way of life. He laid down His life for us, taking our sins upon the cross, so that we, if we confess our sins and believe on Him, will have this abundant and everlasting life. It is so simple—finding this true and fulfilling life— yet so many people strive for all the trappings of this world and never seem to realize that it all leads to a dead end. The gate is too narrow to allow us to carry our possessions with us. All material security must be left behind. He is rest for the weary, strength for the weak, light for the troubled, com- fort for the bereaved and companionship for the lonely. Only life with Christ, through belief in Him, can give us lasting peace and contentment.

SMALL IS THE GATE AND NARROW THE ROAD THAT LEADS TO LIFE

If we would find God amid all the religious externals we must first determine to find Him, and then proceed in the way of simplicity. Now as always God discovers Himself to "babes" and hides Himself in thick darkness from the wise and the prudent. We must simplify our approach to Him. We must strip down to essentials (and they will be found to be blessedly few). We must put away all effort to impress, and come with the guileless candor of childhood. If we do this, without doubt God will quickly respond.

A. W. TOZER
The Pursuit of God

As soon as He finds you ready,
God is bound to act,
bound to pour Himself into your being,
just as, when the air is pure and clear,
the sun must pour into it without holding back.

MEISTER ECKHART
Sermons

Abandon yourself to His care and guidance, as a sheep in the care of a shepherd, and trust Him utterly—no matter if you may seem to yourself to be in the very midst of a desert, with nothing green about you inwardly or outwardly, and may think you will have to make a long journey before you can get into the green pastures. Our Shepherd will turn that very place where you are into green pastures, for He has power to make the desert rejoice and blossom as a rose.

UNKNOWN

No one can serve two masters.
Either he will hate the one and love the other,
or he will be devoted to the one and despise the other.
You cannot serve both God and Money."

MATTHEW 6:24

Empty yourself if you wish to be filled. Go forth, if you wish to enter in," says St. Augustine.

When a man thus clears the ground and makes his soul ready, without doubt God must fill up the void. The very heavens would fall down to fill up empty space, and God will not allow you to remain empty, for that would be against His nature, His attributes; yes, and against His justice. If, therefore, you will be silent, the Word of this Divine birth shall speak in you and shall be heard; but, if you speak, be sure He will be silent. You cannot serve the Word better than by being silent and by listening. If you go out of self, He without doubt will go in, and so it will be much or little of His entering in, according to much or little of your going out.

JOHANNES TAULER
Sermons and Conferences

Know of a truth that if your own honor is of more importance to you and dearer than that of another man, you do wrongfully. Know this, that if you seek something that is your own, you seek not God only; and you will never find Him.

JOHANNES TAULER
Thirty-Seven Sermons for Festivals

*You will seek me and find me
when you seek me with all your heart."*

JEREMIAH 29:13

A spiritual kingdom lies all about us,
enclosing us, embracing us,
altogether within reach of our inner selves,
waiting for us to recognize it.
God Himself is here waiting
our response to His presence.
This eternal world will come alive to us
the moment we begin to reckon
upon its reality.

A. W. TOZER
The Pursuit of God

*Ask and you will receive,
and your joy will be complete."*

JOHN 16:24

Remember that religious truth can never be ascertained by mere speculation. It is largely truth of experience and can only find entrance to the mind through the life. It is heat as well as light, and you must suffer it to warm the heart as well as your reason. Take therefore the character of Christ as delineated in the Gospels, and the character of God as Christ has unfolded it in His teaching and reverently study them, asking yourself all the while what relation you sustain to these persons and whether there is in your heart and life any room for such a friendship as that which Christ offers, any need of such a salvation as He has provided, any witness to the truth of which His life is the revelation. I think that when you come to study carefully first your own moral condition, and then the person and work of Jesus Christ, you will find a marvelous correlation between them, and that you will be convinced that He is indeed the very Friend you need. If you will then commit yourself to Him as your Savior and your Guide, you will soon find the way out of your bewilderment.

WASHINGTON GLADDEN
The Christian Way

All the doors that lead inward,
to the sacred place of the Most High,
are doors outward—
out of self, out of smallness, out of wrong.

GEORGE MACDONALD

To every soul there openeth
A high way and a low;
The low soul gropes the low,
And in between, on the misty flats,
The rest drift to and fro.

To every soul there openeth
A high way and a low;
And every man decideth
Which way his soul shall go.

JOHN OXENHAM

If the soul is to know God it must forget itself and lose itself, for as long as it contemplates self, it cannot contemplate God. When it has lost itself and everything in God, it finds itself again in God when it attains to the knowledge of Him, and it finds also everything which it had abandoned complete in God. MEISTER ECKHART

Sermons

*But though we cannot by our own act
lift ourselves out of the pit,
we must by an act of our own take hold of
the hand which offers us out of it.*

J. C. AND AUGUSTUS HARE
Guesses at Truth

God has strewn all along the way. . .flowers out of His own garden. Behold how the promises, invitations, calls, and encouragements, like lilies, lie around you! Be careful that you do not tread them under foot, sinner. With promises, did God say? Yes, God has mixed all those promises with His own name and His Son's name; which is also the name of mercy, goodness, compassion, love, pity, grace, forgiveness, pardon for the coming sinner to be encouraged! . . . Well, all these things are the good hand of your God upon you, to constrain, to provoke, and to make you willing and able to come, that you might in the end be saved.

WILLIAM H. HARDING

There is but one way to
tranquillity of mind and happiness,
and that is to account
no external things your own,
but to commit all to God.

EPICTETUS

A humble knowledge of thyself is
a surer way to God than
a deep search after learning.

THOMAS À KEMPIS
The Imitation of Christ

We must wait for God,
long, meekly, in the wind and wet,
in the thunder and lightning,
in the cold and the dark.
Wait, and He will come.
He never comes to those who do not wait.

FREDERICK W. FABER

If God had wished to overcome the obstinacy of the most hardened, He could have done so by revealing Himself to them so plainly that they could not doubt the truth of His essence, as He will appear on the last day with such thunder and lightning and such convulsions of nature that the dead will rise up and the blindest will see Him.

This is not the way He wished to appear when He came in mildness because so many had shown themselves unworthy of this clemency that He wished to deprive them of the good they did not desire. It was therefore not right that He should appear in a manner manifestly divine and absolutely capable of convincing everyone, but neither was it right that His coming should be so hidden that He could not be recognized by those who sincerely sought Him. He wished to make Himself perfectly recognizable to them.

Thus wishing to appear openly to those who seek Him with all their heart and hidden from those who shun Him with all their heart, He has qualified our knowledge of Him by giving signs which can be seen by those who seek Him and not by those who do not. There is enough light for those who desire only to see, and enough darkness for those of a contrary disposition.

BLAISE PASCAL
Pensees

Withhold your heart from all things:
seek God, and you shall find Him.

TERESA OF AVILA
Maxims

JESUS CAME TO SHOW US THE WAY

If anyone would come after me,
he must deny himself and
take up his cross and follow me.
For whoever wants to save his life will lose it,
but whoever loses his life for me will find it.
What good will it be for a man if
he gains the whole world,
yet forfeits his soul?"

MATTHEW 16:24–26

All that has here been said, Christ taught in words and fulfilled in works for three and thirty years, and He teacheth it to us very briefly when He saith: "Follow me." But he who will follow Him must forsake all things, for He renounced all things so utterly as no man else hath ever done.

THEOLOGIA GERMANICA

No man comes into the way of Jesus by sheer accident. It is so narrow that no man can see it unless he is deliberately searching for it. To get into the broad road just do nothing or be natural and you will fall into it; but to get into the narrow way you must search diligently. This does not mean that one gets into the way of salvation by effort or efforts in the realm of good works, but it does mean that one must deliberately act upon his own will to come to Christ. It cannot be done without our being conscious of it, nor can it be done without a deliberate act of our own will. C. E. COLTON
The Sermon on the Mount

Jesus is not the door into a little life. He leads us into the largest, fullest life. The Christian sees the King in His beauty in the land of the far distances. And what is our life for, but to make it sacred to Jesus, a life like his, laid down for the good of men? To live for ourselves is to die. To make life an end in itself is to end life; to love your life is to lose it. But lose your life, and you save it; lay it down all at once, if God should so will, or a little at a time every day, for Jesus' sake and the Gospel's, and you will find it lifted up in power to draw men to Jesus.

MALTBIE D. BABCOCK
Thoughts for Every-Day Living

Whatever you may possess,
and however fruitful your activities,
regard them all as worthless
without the inward certainty
and experience of Jesus' love.

The Cloud of Unknowing

*I am the way and the truth and the life.
No one comes to the Father except through me."*

John 14:6

But these are written that you may
believe that Jesus is the Christ,
the Son of God,
and that by believing you may have
life in his name.

John 20:31

Jesus Christ was simplicity itself; always the same, without any affectation in His speech or actions. He taught, with the authority of God made Man, the most sublime truths, and things which had before been unknown. But He propounded His doctrine in a simple, familiar manner, without any pomp or human eloquence, and so that all minds could understand Him. His miracles divine in themselves, are still more divine from the way in which He wrought them.

JEAN-NICOLAS GROU
Manual for Interior Souls

How solemn is that sentence of Christ, "And I, if I be lifted up from the earth, will draw all men unto me"! Not while He lived; not by His direct force, but only when pierced, broken, slain, buried, should His influence issue forth, and death should become the throne of His power. So will it be with us if we are Christ's. Paradoxes upon this truth lie all through the New Testament, and one may walk on them, like stepping stones, from side to side. Sorrow is joy. Death is life. Down is up. Weakness is strength. Loss is gain. Defeat is victory. The world's mightiest men, the very monarchs of its joy, were they who died deaths daily.

HENRY WARD BEECHER
Life Thoughts

*I am the gate;
whoever enters through me will be saved."*

JOHN 10:9

The impression of "authority," and of an authority of an altogether unique kind, produced by His earlier ministry is deepened as His teaching becomes fuller and more explicit. There is a new accent in all His words, even in the simplest of them; and there are passages in His discourses in which He assumes prerogatives and powers such as no prophet had ever claimed before. He forgives the sins of men. He calls to Himself all that labor and are heavy laden, and promises that He will give them rest. He declares that where two or three are gathered together in His name, He is in the midst of them. He has come to lay down His life for the sheep, and they are to become one flock under one Shepherd. To all that listen to His voice and follow Him He gives eternal life; and He says that they shall "never perish, and no one shall snatch them out of My hand." The life which He gives is not given once for all; those who receive it are continuously dependent upon Him; "apart" from Him they wither and die, like the branches apart from the vine. He Himself is "The Way, the Truth, and the Life"; "no one cometh to the Father" but by Him. He is in the Father, and the Father is in Him.

R. W. DALE
*The Living Christ and
the Four Gospels*

*Surely I am with you always,
to the very end of the age."*

MATTHEW 28:20

Christ appeared not as a philosopher or a doctor of many words, or as one who disputes noisily, nor yet as a scribe renowned for wisdom and learning; but in the utmost simplicity did He talk with people, showing unto them the way of truth in His life, His virtues, and His miracles.

ANGELA OF FOLIGNO

He shed tears for those that shed His blood.

THOMAS WATSON

Alexander, Caesar, Charlemagne, and I myself have founded empires; but upon what do these creations of our genius depend? Upon force. Jesus alone founded His empire upon love; and to this very day millions would die for Him.

NAPOLEON BONAPARTE,
conversation with GENERAL BERTRAND
at St.Helena

And He departed from our sight
that He might return to our heart,
and there find Him.
For He departed, and behold,
He is here.

AUGUSTINE OF HIPPO
Confessions

Jesus of Nazareth, without money and arms, conquered more millions than Alexander, Caesar, Mohammed, and Napoleon; without science and learning, He shed more light on things human and divine than all the philosophers and scholars combined; without the eloquence of the school, He spoke words of life such as were never spoken before, nor since, and produced effects which lie beyond the reach of orator or poet; without writing a single line, He has set more pens in motion and furnished themes for more sermons, orations, discussions, works of art, learned volumes, and sweet songs of praise than the whole army of great men of ancient and modern times. Born in a manger and crucified as a malefactor, He now controls the destinies of the civilized world, and rules a spiritual empire which embraces one third of the inhabitants of the globe.   Phillip Schaff

Truth lies in character.
Christ did not simply speak the truth;
He was Truth—Truth through and through,
for truth is a thing not of words
but of life and being.

Frederick W. Robertson

*Jesus Christ is the same
yesterday and today and forever.*

HEBREWS 13:8

Christianity is not a theory or speculation,
but a life, not a philosophy of life,
but a living presence.

SAMUEL TAYLOR COLERIDGE

The teachings of Jesus are profound. The way to inner power lies in the realization of helplessness. The way to salvation is through confession and acknowledgment of sin. Leadership is found in becoming the servant of all. The way to knowledge of God begins with the admission of ignorance. The way to independence lies through dependence on God, the way to true freedom lies in surrendering to God, the way to find self is to give up self. In Jesus' life of service, He rejected the traditional concept of power and position. He treated women with respect and insisted upon washing His disciples' feet. His whole life was a testimony of service and submission.   C. M. M.

The words of our Lord shine by their own light, they carry with them their own credentials. Like the person who uttered them, they are unique. They are simple, yet profound, calm yet intense, "mild yet terrible." They have a peculiar force which expresses authority. They do not persuade or entreat or reason with the hearer: They penetrate, they convict, they reveal. The charm and the wonder of them are as fresh today, for the unlearned as well as for the learned, as when the people were astonished at His doctrine.   ARCHBISHOP OF ARMAGH
(DR. D'ARCY)
Ruling Ideas of Our Lord

The parables of Jesus are like great art.
They express a profound simplicity.
The familiar stories yield new vistas of thought
each time they are explored.
But you can never get all that is there.

DOUGLAS BEYER
Parables for Christian Living

Supposing one single man to have left a book of predictions concerning Jesus Christ as to the time and manner of His coming, and supposing him to have come agreeably to these predictions, the argument would be of almost infinite force; yet here the evidence is stronger beyond all comparison; a succession of men for the space of four thousand years follow one another, without interruption or variation, in foretelling the same great event. A whole people are the harbingers of the Messiah, and such a people as subsisted four thousand years to testify in a general body their assured hope and expectation, from which no severity of threats or persecutions could oblige them to depart. This is a case which challenges in a far more transcendent degree our assent and wonder.   BLAISE PASCAL

Pensees

CLOSING PRAYER

Lord Jesus Christ,
You have said that You are the way,
the truth, and the life.
Suffer us not to stray from You,
who are the way,
nor to distrust You, who are the truth,
nor to rest in anything other than You,
who are the life;
beyond which there is nothing to be desired,
neither in heaven, nor in earth;
for Your Name's sake. Amen.

CHRISTIAN PRAYER (1578)

PART TWO

THE PONDERING SOUL—
ENCOURAGEMENT TO ACCEPT
GOD'S CALL

I stood there in a lovely garden one night—
And marveled at the enchanting sight!
When lo! There in the cathedral-like hush
I heard the swish of a painter's brush.
I saw the flowers and trees in prayer.
And knew the Great Gardener was working there!

FRANCES ANGERMAYER

CHAPTER 4

We Are Often Blind to God's Presence All Around Us

The light shines in the darkness,
but the darkness has not understood it.

John 1:5

God uses simple things and ordinary moments to reveal Himself to us, if only we had the eyes to see and the ears to hear Him. Everything has meaning because everything speaks of God and points toward God. When we see God everywhere, our faith in Him grows deeper. We can see Him in the sunrise and in the sunset, in the rainbow and in the storm clouds, in smiles and in tears, in the humblest wayside flower and in the face of our neighbor. God is always present, but often we are not aware of

Him because we are so busy running here and there, so occupied with daily matters, that we have become deaf to His voice calling us, guiding us day by day along the path He has chosen for us. Something has to happen to release us from our absorption in self. Sometimes events will do it. We may encounter God in a crisis that brings us to our senses. Sometimes we are quiet enough to hear God's voice whispering in our ears, "I am the Way." When sadness comes, the one who can see God's hand at work will have peace. Hearing and seeing are inner senses as well as outer senses.

GOD IS THERE.
WE JUST NEED TO
OPEN OUR EYES AND SEE

To us also through every star,
through every blade of grass,
is not God made visible if
we will open our minds and eyes?

THOMAS CARLYLE

We are living in a world of beauty,
but few of us open our eyes to see it:
What a different place this world would be
if your senses were trained to see and to hear!

LORADO TAFT

Earth's crammed with heaven,
And every common bush afire with God;
But only he who sees, takes off his shoes,
The rest sit round it and pluck blackberries.

ELIZABETH BARRETT BROWNING,
from *Aurora Leigh*

If we do not see Him,
it is not because He is not here,
but because we are spiritually blind.

W. TALIAFERRO THOMPSON

For behold the Word, which is the Wisdom of God, is in your heart as a Light unto your feet and lantern unto your paths. It is as a speaking Word of God in your soul; and as soon as you are ready to hear, this eternal speaking Word will speak Wisdom and Love in your inward parts and bring forth the birth of Christ, with all His holy nature, spirit, and tempers, within you.

WILLIAM LAW

God is always here, wherever we are.
But consciousness is so occupied with other matters
that it is not aware of Him.
Or consciousness is so dulled by its
habitual occupations that it cannot perceive Him.

ALBERT E. DAY
Autobiography of Prayer

There are some things that must be spiritually discerned and appreciated, and if eyes are blind, and heart is dull and the soul desensitized, no wonder it is difficult to appreciate the higher things of God.

JONATHAN SWIFT

If a man could make a single rose
we should give him an empire;
yet roses and flowers no less beautiful
are scattered in profusion over the world,
and no one regards them.

MARTIN LUTHER

If God is present at every point in space, if we cannot go where He is not, cannot even conceive of a place where He is not, why then has not that Presence become the one universally celebrated fact of the world? The patriarch Jacob, "in waste howling wilderness," gave the answer to that question. He saw a vision of God and cried out in wonder, "Surely the Lord is in this place; and I knew it not."

A. W. TOZER
The Pursuit of God

So present in this world,
Dear God, so loud its din,
We seldom hear the voice
That speaks within!

RALPH S. CUSHMAN

God broadcasts His messages and only those whose instruments are rightly tuned can receive them. He seeks to reveal Himself all the time, and the difference of reception lies not with Him but with us.   MAUD ROYDEN

Events, compounded as they are of people and circumstances, offer the same possibility of finding God's meaning. They are like windows open in to the very room where His plans are spread; we are welcome to look in over His shoulder and catch a little glimpse of what He has in mind.

MARGUERITE HARMON BRO
More Than We Are

Oh, my God, how does it happen in this poor old world, that Thou art so great and yet nobody feels Thee, that Thou givest Thyself to everybody and nobody knows Thy name! Men flee from Thee and say they cannot find Thee; they turn their backs and say they cannot see Thee; they stop their ears and say they cannot hear Thee!

HANS DENCK
On the Law of God

Blessed are they that have eyes to see,
They shall find God everywhere.
They shall see Him where others see stones.

Blessed are they that see visions.
They shall rejoice in the hidden ways of God.

JOHN OXENHAM
from "Some Blessings"

If the great things of religion are rightly under-stood they will affect the heart. The reason men are not affected by such infinitely great, important, glorious, and wonderful things, as they often heard read of in the Word of God, is, undoubtedly, because they are blind; if they were not so, it would be impossible, and utterly inconsistent with human nature that their hearts should be otherwise than strongly impressed, and greatly moved by such things. JONATHAN EDWARDS
The Works of President Edwards

Our eyes shall see thee, which before saw dust.

GEORGE HERBERT

The world around us is the mighty volume wherein God hath declared Himself. Human languages and characters are different in different nations, and those of one nation are not understood by the rest. But the book of nature is written in an universal character, which every man may read in his own language.   JOHN WESLEY

Letters

*Grant I may so
Thy steps track here below
That in these masques and shadows I may see
Thy sacred way,
And by those hid ascents climb to that day
Which breaks from Thee,
Who art in all things though invisibly.*

HENRY VAUGHN

Marks of glory are upon all things, and the marks are cruciform and blood-stained. And one sighs, like the convinced Thomas of old, "My Lord and my God" (John 20:28). Dare one lift one's eyes and look? Nay, whither can one look and not see Him? For field and stream and teeming streets are full of Him.   THOMAS R. KELLY

A Testament of Devotion

It is surprising how easy it is to hear music
in the waves and songs in the wild whisperings
of the winds; to see God everywhere in the stones,
in the rocks, in the rippling brooks,
and hear Him everywhere, in the lowing of cattle,
in the rolling of thunder, and in the fury of tempests.

CHARLES H. SPURGEON
Sermons

Can you sit on top of a hill in spring,
And watch the birds sailing by on the wing,
And see the clouds drifting in the sky,
And doubt there's a God who dwells on high?

UNKNOWN

How we go through life,
losing most of the beauties of it
from sheer inability to see.

DAVID GRAYSON
Great Possessions

Still, Thou art hidden, O Lord, from my soul in Thy light and Thy blessedness; and therefore my soul still walks in darkness and wretchedness. For it looks, and does not see Thy beauty. It hearkens, and does not hear Thy harmony. It smells, and does not perceive Thy fragrance. It tastes, and does not recognize Thy sweetness. It touches, and does not feel Thy pleasantness. ANSELM OF CANTERBURY, from the Latin translation of *Proslogium, Monologium* by SIDNEY NORTON DEANE

There are some who pass through life
as through a tunnel,
without ever understanding the
splendor and the security and
the warmth of the sun of faith.

JOSE ESCRIVA

How great and amiable He is in His mysteries! But we have not the eyes to see them, and we lack the sensitiveness to see God in everything.

FRANCOIS FENELON
Instructions

MY LORD IS NEAR ME
ALL THE TIME

In the lightning flash across the sky
His mighty power I see,
And I know if He can reign on high,
His light can shine on me.
I've seen it in the lightning,
Heard it in the thunder,
And felt it in the rain.
My Lord is near me all the time.

BARBARA FOWLER GAULTNEY

There is hardly ever a complete silence in our soul.
God is whispering to us well nigh incessantly.
Whenever the sounds of the world die out in the
soul, or sink low, then we hear these whisperings of
God. He is always whispering to us, only we do not
always hear, because of the noise, hurry, and dis-
traction which life causes as it rushes on.

FREDERICK W. FABER

God is not external to anyone,
but is present with all things,
though they are ignorant that He is so.

PLOTINUS
Ennead

CLOSING PRAYER

God and Father,
I repent of my sinful preoccupation
with visible things.
The world has been too much with me.
Thou has been here and I knew it not.
I have been blind to Thy presence.
Open my eyes that I may
behold Thee in and around me.
For Christ's sake, Amen.

A. W. TOZER
The Pursuit of God

CHAPTER 5

EVERYTHING THAT HAPPENS IN THE WORLD IS PART OF GOD'S GREAT PLAN, RUNNING THROUGH ALL ETERNITY

The fool says in his heart,
"There is no God."

PSALM 14:1

Go out into a garden and examine a seed; examine the same plant in the bud and in the fruit, and you must confess the whole process is a miracle, a perpetual miracle. Take it at any period, make yourself as familiar with all the facts as you can at each period, and in each explanation there will be some step or appearance to be referred directly to the Great Creator; something not the effect of the sower's deposit, nor of the waterer's hope. It is not the loam, nor the gravel, it is not the furrow of the ploughshare, nor the glare of the sun that calls greenness from the dust, it is the present power of Him who said, "Seed-time and harvest shall not fail." Needs there, my brethren, any other book than this returning summer that reminds us of the first creation, to suggest the Presence of God?

RALPH WALDO EMERSON

THE KNOWLEDGE OF GOD GIVES LIFE ITS UNITY AND MEANING

The mystery of the universe
and the meaning of God's world
are shrouded in hopeless obscurity
until we learn to feel that all laws
suppose a lawgiver and that all working
involves a divine energy.

ALEXANDER MACLAREN

The order of the world is not accident. There is nothing actual which could be actual without some measure of order. The religious insight is the grasp of this truth: That the order of the world, the depth of reality of the world,—the beauty of the world, the zest of life, and the mastery of evil, are all bound together—not accidentally, but by reason of this truth; that the universe exhibits a creativity with infinite freedom, and a realm of forms with infinite possibilities; but that this creativity and these forms are together important to achieve actuality apart from the ideal harmony, which is God.

ALFRED NORTH WHITEHEAD

Belief of God is acceptance of the basic principle that the universe makes sense, that there is behind it an ultimate purpose.

CARL WALLACE MILLER

The laws of nature are but the thoughts and agencies of God—the modes in which He works and carries out the designs of His providence and will.

TRYON EDWARDS

*A person's spiritual life is
always dwarfed when
cut apart from history.*

RUFUS M. JONES

Nature imitates herself. A grain thrown into good ground brings forth fruit; a principle thrown into a good mind brings forth fruit. Everything is created and conducted by the same Master,—the root, the branch, the fruits,—the principles, the consequences.   BLAISE PASCAL
Pensees

*The universe is but one great city,
full of beloved ones, divine and human by nature,
endeared to each other.*

EPICTETUS
Discourses

Once I found a friend. "Dear me," I said, "he was made for me." But now I find more and more friends who seem to have been made for me, and more and yet more made for me. Is it possible we were all made for each other all over the world?

GILBERT K. CHESTERTON
The Notebook

O God, whose laws will never change,
We thank Thee for these things we know:
That after rain the sun will shine;
That after darkness, light appears;
That winter always brings the spring;
That after sleep, we wake again;
That life goes on and love remains,
And life and love can never die.

JEANETTE E. PERKINS

The body is a unit, though it is made up of many parts; and though all its parts are many, they form one body. So it is with Christ. For we were all baptized by one Spirit into one body—whether Jews or Greeks, slave or free—and we were all given the one Spirit to drink.

Now the body is not made up of one part but of many. If the foot should say, "Because I am not a hand, I do not belong to the body," it would not for that reason cease to be part of the body. And if the ear should say, "Because I am not an eye, I do not belong to the body," it would not for that reason cease to be part of the body. If the whole body were an eye, where would the sense of hearing be? If the whole body were an ear, where would the sense of smell be? But in fact God has arranged the parts in the body, every one of them, just as he wanted them to be. If they were all one part, where would the body be? As it is, there are many parts, but one body.

The eye cannot say to the hand, "I don't need you!" And the head cannot say to the feet, "I don't need you!" On the contrary, those parts of the body that seem to be weaker are indispensable, and the parts that we think are less honorable we treat with special honor. And the parts that are unpresentable are treated with special modesty, while our presentable parts need no special treatment. But God has combined the members of the body and has given greater honor to the parts that lacked it, so that there should be no division in the body, but that its parts should have equal concern for each other. If one part suffers, every part suffers with it; if one part is honored, every part rejoices with it.

Now you are the body of Christ, and each one of you is a part of it.

1 Corinthians 12:12–27

There Is Evidence of God All Around Us

When men shout that "God is dead," this can only mean that He is not in the place where they are looking for Him.

W. A. Visser
quoted in *The New York Times*,
December 20, 1965

This is a piece too fair
To be the child of Chance, and not of Care.
No atoms casually together hurl'd
Could e'er produce so beautiful a world.

JOHN DRYDEN

The monumental evidence of God is, I believe, the fact of spiritual personality through which divine traits of character are revealed. Stars and mountains and ordered processes of nature reveal law and mathematics and beauty, but they reveal and can reveal no traits of character, no qualities of personality, no warmth and intimacy of heart and mind. If we are ever to be convinced that self-giving love is a reality of God's nature, we shall be convinced by seeing this love break through some human organ of His Spirit. . . . As the sap flows through the branches of the vine and vitalizes the whole organism so that it bursts into the beauty and glory of foliage and blossom and finally into fruit, so through the lives of men and women, inwardly responsive and joyously receptive, the life of God as Spirit flows, carrying vitality, awakening love, creating passion for goodness, kindling the fervor of consecration and producing that living body, that organism of the Spirit, that "blessed community," which continues through the centuries as the revelation of God as love and tenderness and eternal goodness.   RUFUS M. JONES

There can be no doubt but that everything in the world, by the beauty of its order, and the evidence of a determinate and beneficial purpose which pervades it, testifies that some supreme efficient power must have preexisted, by which the whole was ordained for a specific end.

JOHN MILTON
A Treatise on Christian Doctrine

We do not have to go to the universe to prove the existence of God from design. We do not have to dig down into the bowels of the earth, nor go up to the stars for proofs of the divine existence. He is not far from every one of us. As Paul says, "In Him we move and have our being," and as Tennyson says, "Closer is He than breathing; and nearer than hands and feet." God is here. There is no escaping Him.   CHARLES H. PARKHURST

*The earth, the sun and stars,
and the universe itself;
and the charming variety of the seasons,
demonstrate the existence of a Divinity.*

PLATO
De Legibus

The demand for proof of Jesus' teachings is like a demand made upon a once-blind man, to give proofs of how and why he sees light. The blind man whose sight was restored, still the same man he was before, can only say, he was blind, but now sees. Just this, and nothing else, can one answer who formerly did not understand the meaning of life, but now does good in life, but now he knows. The once-blind man, when told he is cured not according to rule, and that he who cured him is the evil-doer, and that he must be cured in another way, can only reply, that he knows nothing as to the correctness of the manner of cure, or as to the faultiness of his healer, or as to there being a better way of cure, but that he knows only, he was blind, and now sees. And just so, he who grasps the meaning of this doctrine, that the true good is to fulfill the Father's will, can say nothing as to the regularity of the teaching, or as to the possibility of gaining something better. He will say: "Formerly I did not see the meaning of life; now I see. I know no more."

And Jesus said: "My teaching is the awakening of the life which has so far slept; he who will believe my teaching, shall awaken to eternal life, and continue to live after death. My teaching is not proven in any way, except that men give themselves up to it, because it alone has the promise of life for men."

LEO TOLSTOY
The Collected Works of Leo Tolstoy

*The best that man can invent or discover is
only a pale reminder of what
God has done through the ages.*

ALEXANDER MACLAREN

MIRACLES ARE SIMPLY
THE EVIDENCE OF THE PRESENCE OF GOD

Every moment of this strange and lovely life from dawn to dusk, is a miracle. Somewhere, always, a rose is opening its petals to the dawn. Somewhere, always, a flower is fading in the dusk. The incense that rises with the sun, and the scents that die in the dark, are all gathered, sooner or later, into the solitary fragrance that is God. Faintly, elusively, that fragrance lingers over all of us.

BEVERLEY NICHOLS
The Fool Hath Said

Miracles are not in contradiction to nature. They are only in contradiction with what we know of nature.

AUGUSTINE OF HIPPO

The genuine realist, if he is an unbeliever, will always find strength and ability to disbelieve in the miraculous, and if he is confronted with a miracle as an irrefutable fact he would rather disbelieve his own senses than admit the fact. Faith does not. . . spring from the miracle, but the miracle from faith.

FYODOR DOSTOEVSKY

*How great are his signs,
how mighty his wonders!*

DANIEL 4:3

A mouse is miracle enough
to stagger sextillions of infidels.

WALT WHITMAN,
from "Song of Myself"

*Tiger, tiger, burning bright
In the forests of the night,
What immortal hand or eye
Could frame thy fearful symmetry?*

WILLIAM BLAKE
from "The Tiger"

If they do not listen to
Moses and the Prophets,
they will not be convinced
even if someone rises from the dead."

LUKE 16:31

*He who draws near to God
one step through doubtings dim
God will advance a mile
in blazing light to him.*

AUTHOR UNKNOWN

CLOSING PRAYER

*Almighty God,
Lord of the storm and of the calm,
of day and night, of life and death,
I pray that You will keep my heart
steadfast upon Your faithfulness,
that I may continually see the miraculous
in the world about me and
in the changed lives of those who have found
the magnificent freedom in following You.
Amen.*

PART THREE

THE AWAKENING SOUL— FINDING THE PEARL OF GREAT PRICE

The word of God came unto me,
Sitting alone among the multitudes:
And my blind eyes were touched with light,
And there was laid upon my lips a flame of fire.

HELEN KELLER

CHAPTER 6

One Thing I Do Know:
I Was Blind, But Now I See

*"My ears had heard of you
but now my eyes have seen you."*

JOB 42:5

Throughout the ages God has revealed Himself to man and set aflame the fire of faith in his soul and imparted to him the truth that will set him free. This call of God may come as a clap of thunder in overwhelming holiness or simply in a glimpse of His Presence in a quiet moment: in a stranger's eyes, in the clear evening violet sky, in a poem by Whittier, in the calm, peaceful sunrise, in an awakening rosebud, or in the death of a loved one. However it may happen, we open ourselves to

God, His Presence enters and takes possession of our hearts and there He establishes His kingdom. We and He become One. We will never be the same again. Something supernatural has happened—something that is inexpressible and undeniable, something that makes life worthwhile.

YIELDING TO GOD IS THE BEGINNING

Taste and see that the LORD is good; blessed is the man who takes refuge in him. Fear the LORD, you his saints, for those who fear him lack nothing.

PSALM 34:8–9

When man humbles himself, God cannot restrain His mercy; He must come down and pour His grace into the humble man, and He gives Himself most of all, and all at once, to the least of all. It is essential to God to give, for His essence is His goodness and His goodness is His love. Love is the root of all joy and sorrow.

MEISTER ECKHART
Sermons

*To have found God is not an end in itself,
but a beginning.*

FRANZ ROSENSWEIG

We require great confidence
to abandon ourselves,
without any reserve, to Divine Providence;
but when we do abandon all,
Our Lord takes care of all, and disposes of all.

FRANCIS DE SALES
Consoling Thoughts

*I waited patiently for the LORD;
he turned to me and heard my cry.*

PSALM 40:1

And first an hour of mournful musing,
And then a gush of bitter tears.
And then a dreary calm diffusing
Its deadly mist o'er joys and cares;
And then a breathing from above,
And then a star in heaven brightening—
The star, the glorious star of love.

EMILY BRONTË

When we recognize His Presence and invite Him to come in and sup with us, and we with Him, what joy it is! We have been found by God. We had hints all along, but when we finally opened our eyes and beheld, what a miracle it seemed to be! It was like finding an oasis in the desert, a pot of gold at the end of the rainbow, a pearl in the oyster.

C. M. M.

And then all her former fear falls away,
and she knows clearly that she is free,
and sings with joy to see herself
in such serene and tranquil peace.

JOHN OF THE CROSS
The Dark Night of the Soul

You sit in prayer, perhaps reading the Scriptures, perhaps not. When in a secret instant, you unexpectedly yield your inmost Self to God as He receives you into Himself. In the moment of rediscovered union you silently cry out from the depths of your heart: "Why have I been so foolish not to realize that everything in me desires the fulfillment of the union with You and nothing else, absolutely nothing else. For this is what I desire to be. This is who I truly am—one marked, claimed and surrendered to Your love."

JAMES FINLEY
The Awakening Call

He only asks you to yield yourself to Him, that He may work in you to will and to do by His own mighty power. Your part is to yield yourself, His part is to work; and never, never will He give you any command which is not accompanied by ample power to obey it. Take no thought for the morrow in this matter, but abandon yourself with a generous trust to our loving Lord, who has promised never to call His own sheep out into any path without Himself going before them to make the way easy and safe. Take each little step as He makes it plain to you.

HANNAH WHITALL SMITH
The Christian's Secret of a Happy Life

THEIR EYES WERE OPENED
AND THEY RECOGNIZED HIM

I am sending you to them to open their eyes and turn them from darkness to light, and from the power of Satan to God, so that they may receive forgiveness of sins and a place among those who are sanctified by faith in me."   ACTS 26:17–18

He brought light out of darkness, not out of lesser light; He can bring thy summer out of winter, though thou have no spring; though in the ways of fortune or understanding or conscience, thou have benighted till now, wintered and frozen, clouded and eclipsed, dampened and benumbed, smothered and stupified till now, now God comes to thee, not as in the dawning of the day, not as in the bud of the spring, but as the sun at noon.

JOHN DONNE

Open my eyes that I may see wonderful things.

PSALM 119:18

*O*pen my eyes, that I may see;
Glimpses of truth Thou hast for me;
Place in my hands the wonderful key
That shall unclasp and set me free:
Silently now I wait for Thee,
Ready my God, Thy will to see;
Open my eyes, illumine me,
Spirit divine!

CLARA H. SCOTT

Suddenly, in the midst of great tragedy or joy, through windows hardly noticed before, we catch a glimpse of eternity, and begin to understand that all our life, all our achievement and glory, is as a grain of sand on an endless shore, a single bead in a chain that stretches on and on into infinity.

SAMUEL DRESNER
Three Paths of God and Man

We must understand the true life, what it is. The true life is brought to light always in the lost being brought back to where they belong, in the awakening of those who slept. People who have the true life, who are restored to the source of their being, cannot, like worldly men, take account of others as better or worse but, being sharers of the Father's life, they can take delight only in the return of the lost to their Father.   LEO TOLSTOY
The Collected Works of Leo Tolstoy

This experience of God is the only thing which is certain and self-evident. Before his heart has been moved in this manner, a man is deaf and blind towards everything, even towards miracles. But once this interior sense of God has come to him, he needs no other miracle than that which has been accomplished within his own soul.

ALEXANDER YELCHANINOV
Diary

Amazing grace! How sweet the sound
That saved a wretch like me!
I once was lost, but now am found.
Was blind, but now I see,
'Twas grace that taught my heart to fear
And grace my fears relieved;
How precious did that grace appear
The hour I first believed!

JOHN NEWTON

The landscape bursts into flower. He no longer sees things as a succession but as a pattern; not as a grey blur but as a flaming riot of color; not as the result of a necessary and remote collection of laws in the outcome of which his life is as insignificant as it is unquestioned, but as the spontaneous and unique dispensation of providence whereby he is singled out to enjoy the intimate ecstasies of being alive. He sees the inwardness of creatures as well as the beauties of their outwardness, and, if he has learned the lesson that his experience is meant to teach him, he refers them back again gratefully to God. He, in short, wakes up.

HUBERT VAN ZELLER
We Die Standing Up

For with you is the fountain of life;
in your light we see light.

PSALM 36:9

CLOSING PRAYER

Lord, I am Yours;
I do yield myself up entirely to You,
and I believe that You do take me.
I leave myself with You.
Work in me all the good pleasure of Your will,
and I will only lie still in Your hands and trust You.
Amen.

HANNAH WHITALL SMITH
The Christian's Secret of a Happy Life

CHAPTER 7

THE CONVERSION EXPERIENCE
IS A MYSTERY OF GOD

*"Then you will know the truth,
and the truth will set you free."*

JOHN 8:32

Conversion happens differently and uniquely in each person's life. It is not a change which we bring about in ourselves, but which God brings about in us, only as we permit ourselves to be filled with God's love. Sometimes in a gentle and silent way we become aware of the Spirit of God invading our soul and bringing about an awareness of God's goodness. Sometimes in a sudden burst of fire our souls are engulfed with God's love. Often it happens through a succession of events that lead to our realization of the truth, or in countless other ways—this new life comes to us. Conversion involves a process of growth and change. It begins with God and continues quietly within us throughout our lives through a succession of events, all leading in a single direction, as we seek to please Him. God becomes the center of our life and we begin to see the "vanity of things."

GOD HAS CALLED US OUT OF DARKNESS INTO HIS WONDERFUL LIGHT

I waited patiently for the LORD;
he turned to me and heard my cry.
He lifted me out of the slimy pit,
out of the mud and mire;
he set my feet on a rock
and gave me a firm place to stand.
He put a new song in my mouth,
a hymn of praise to our God.

PSALM 40:1–3

There are no buds which can open without the sun, but there is a great difference in the time it takes them to unfold. Some have their outer petals so closely wrapped and glued together, that there must be many days of warm shining before they will begin to expand; and others there are which make haste to get out of the ground; and almost as soon as they are buds, they are blossoms. So is it with human hearts. Some are so cold and impervious that it seems as though God's Spirit never could reach them; and others there are which open to its first influences. HENRY WARD BEECHER
Life Thoughts

Spiritual awakening can happen at any time from childhood to old age, at any place—in a quiet moment in church or in a busy subway station, gradually or suddenly. We are all so different. God knows how to reveal Himself to each one in a special way, unique to his personality and station in life. The young person may remain silent about the encounter and may even be a little bewildered by it, but one thing is certain; he will not forget. It will remain a high point in his life and he will refer to it from time to time as thoughts of God overcome him. It will be a source of comfort and strength as daily pressures and responsibilities press in upon him. Then later in life as he commits all to God, he will look back upon this initial awakening as the first decisive event of his spiritual journey. God's plan for his life was taking shape during all this time and he is now ready to embrace it wholeheartedly.   C. M. M.

All who call on God in true faith,
earnestly from the heart will certainly be heard,
and will receive what they have asked and desired.

MARTIN LUTHER

Conversion are like the dawn of morning:
They come and eradicate the very dewdrops
and change them to jewels; they wake all the birds;
they wake all the hearts and melodies.

PHILLIPS BROOKS

Conversion is a deep work—a heart work.
It goes throughout the man,
Thoughout the mind, thoughout the members,
thoughout the entire life.

JOSEPH ALLEINE

I thought the old sun shone a good deal brighter than it ever had before—I thought that it was just smiling upon me; and as I walked out upon Boston Common and heard the birds singing in the trees, I thought they were all singing a song to me. . . . It seemed to me that I was in love with all creation. I had not a bitter feeling against any man, and I was ready to take all men to my heart. If a man has not the love of God shed abroad in his heart he has not yet been regenerated.

DWIGHT L. MOODY

Can Christ be in your heart,
and you not know it?
Can one king be dethroned and
another crowned in your soul,
and you hear no scuffle?

WILLIAM GURNALL

Will it come, or will it not,
The day when the joy becomes great,
The day when the grief becomes small?

GUNNAR EKELOF

Then suddenly it happened. I cannot explain it even to this day. It seems so simple and so ordinary. I just bowed my face in my hands and, suddenly, the tears gushed through my fingers and down on to the chair. And all I know is that Jesus Christ, the Savior of the World, came into this heart of mine. I knew as I dried my tears that the great change had taken place, knew it beyond the shadow of a doubt.

That was forty years ago. It has lasted from that day to this, and Jesus Christ means more to me now than He ever did before.

OSWALD J. SMITH

Wake up, O sleeper,
rise from the dead,
and Christ will shine on you."

EPHESIANS 5:14

Whoever finds it has found all that he can desire. Here is the height and the depths; here is the breadth and the length thereof manifested, as fully as ever the capacity of the soul can contain.

JAKOB BOEHME

A new day rose upon me. It was as if another sun had risen into the sky; the heavens were indescribably brighter, and the earth fairer; and that day has gone on brightening to the present hour. I have known the other joys of life, I suppose, as much as most men; I have known art and beauty, music and gladness; I have known friendship and love and family ties; but it is certain that till we see God in the world—God in the bright and boundless universe—we never know the highest joy. It is far more than if one were translated to a world a thousand times fairer than this; for that supreme and central Light of Infinite Love and Wisdom, shining over this world and all worlds, alone can show us how noble and beautiful, how fair and glorious they are.

ORVILLE DEWEY

Christ is my Savior. He is my life. He is everything to me in heaven and earth. Once while traveling in a sandy region I was tired and thirsty. Standing on the top of a mound I looked for water. The sight of a lake at a distance brought joy to me, for now I hoped to quench my thirst. I walked toward it for a long time, but I could never reach it. Afterwards I found out that it was a mirage, only a mere appearance of water caused by the refracted rays of the sun. In reality there was none. In a like manner I was moving about the world in search of the of life. The things of this world—wealth, position, honor and luxury—looked like a lake by drinking of whose waters I hoped to quench my spiritual thirst. But I could never find a drop of water to quench the thirst of my heart. I was dying of thirst. When my spiritual eyes were opened, I saw the rivers of living water flowing from His pierced side. I drank of it and was satisfied. Thirst was no more. Ever since I have always drunk of that water of life, and have never been athirst in the sandy desert of this world. My heart is full of praise.

SADHU SUNDAR SINGH, *The Sadhu,*
by B.H. STREATER and A. J. APPASAMY

I found Him not in world or sun,
Or eagle's wing, or insect's eye;
Nor through the questions men may try,
The petty cobwebs we have spun. . .

A warmth within the breast would melt
The freezing reason's colder part,
And, like a man in wrath, the heart
Stood up and answered, "I have felt!"

ALFRED LORD TENNYSON

My education and surroundings have always been religious. The precise time of my conversion I cannot tell. I never felt that burden of sin which Bunyan describes, and probably never shall. And yet, I cannot for a moment doubt that I am a child of God.

HENRY WARD BEECHER
Autobiographical Reminiscences

The clock of mercy struck in Heaven the hour and moment of my emancipation, for the time had come. Between half-past ten o'clock, when I entered that chapel, and half-past twelve o'clock, when I was back again at home, what a change had taken place in me! I had passed from darkness into marvelous light, from death to life. Simply by looking to Jesus, I had been delivered from despair, and I was brought into such a joyous state of mind that, when they saw me at home, they said to me, "Something wonderful has happened to you"; and I was eager to tell them all about it.

CHARLES H. SPURGEON

God must take the initiative and come to us if we are to experience Him. This is the witness of the entire Bible. He came to Adam and Eve in the Garden of Eden. In love He fellowshipped with them and they with Him. He came to Noah, Abraham, Moses, and the prophets. God took the initiative for each person in the Old Testament to experience Him in a personal fellowship of love. This is true of the New Testament as well. Jesus came to the disciples, and chose them to be with Him and experience His Love. He came to Paul on the Damascus Road. In our natural human state, we do not seek God on our own initiative. "There is no one righteous, not one; there is no one who understands, no one who seeks after God" (Romans 3:10–11).

Henry T. Blackaby and Claude V. King
Experiencing God

I know that Christ is alive,
and personal and real,
and closer than we think.
I have met Him.
I have felt His presence.

Peter Marshall
"The Tap on the Shoulder"

*I could not say I believe,
I know! I have had the experience of
being gripped by something that people call God.*

CARL G. JUNG

After Blaise Pascal's death in 1662, it was discovered that he had stitched a parchment inside his coat, between the cloth and lining, so that it would lie next to his heart. On a paper within this parchment under a cross and the sun with rays rising heavenward, was the year, the day, and the hour of his conversion. Then, in a line by itself, and in big capitals, a single word, "FIRE," and then:

> *"God of Abraham, God of Isaac, God of Jacob
> not of the philosophers and scholars
> I know! I know! I feel! Joy! Peace!"*

Pascal knew the power of faith in God, not because he studied and reasoned, but because he realized what God had done in the lives of others before him who had faith in God. What an earth-shattering discovery that changed his life!

C. M. M.

I heard no outward voices; I saw no external light or vision of any kind; there was no text of Scripture brought to my mind; neither did I feel any exterior joy. I received a conviction or evidence in my soul whereby I was assured that my sins were forgiven, for Christ's sake, and that I was accepted of God in the Beloved. Thomas Rutherford

He who began a good work in you
will carry it on to completion
until the day of Christ Jesus.

Philippians 1:6

Closing Prayer

*Father, You who are full of compassion,
I commit and commend myself unto You.
Be the goal of my pilgrimage,
and my rest by the way.
Let my soul take refuge from the
crowding turmoil of worldly thoughts
beneath the shadow of Your wings;
let my heart find peace in You, O God. Amen.*

Augustine of Hippo

CHAPTER 8

KNOWING GOD IS
THE ULTIMATE EXPERIENCE IN LIFE

"Whoever drinks the water
I give him will never thirst.
Indeed, the water I give him will become in him
a spring of water welling up to eternal life."

JOHN 4:14

If we have experienced God in our lives, we can never again be the same. Anything of this earth will fail to satisfy us. We have a new outlook which gives new life to whatever we may be doing. We know that each day's problems will be solved spiritually. Truth will shine in us and we will be able to hear God's clear voice. We have been with God and no longer think in the same way. Our desires are new and the old things have lost their power to attract us. The whole experience is a gift from God and is unexplainable and incomprehensible to one who has not experienced it. We realize that the only thing that really matters, that is absolutely necessary, is this new life in Christ. All else, even though good and beautiful in its time and place, is mere froth.

EVERYTHING HAS NEW MEANING

As we begin to focus upon God, the things of the spirit will take shape before our inner eyes. Obedience to the word of Christ will bring an inward revelation of the Godhead (John 14:21–23). It will give acute perception enabling us to see God even as is promised to the pure in heart. A new God-consciousness will seize upon us and we shall begin to taste and hear and inwardly feel God, who is our life and our all. There will be seen the constant shining of "the true Light that gives light to every man that was coming into the world" (John 1:9). More and more, as our faculties grow sharper and more sure, God will become to us the great All, and His presence the glory and wonder of our lives.

A. W. TOZER
The Pursuit of God

To the soul that is wholly bent upon God a thousand fretting cares and vexing problems which tear the lives of others in pieces simply cease to exist. With the submerging of the irrelevant, the soul is free to give itself to that which really matters.

EMILY HERMAN
Creative Prayer

Once one has encountered God everything is changed. One does not lead a charmed life—but it is amazing how charming the commonplace can become. One still has heavy work to do but one works with assurance and poise. One still has temptations to meet but they have been robbed of most of their power. One runs into adversity but the inner certainty remains.

ALBERT E. DAY
An Autobiography of Prayer

*To fall in love with God is
the greatest of all romances;
To seek Him, the greatest adventure;
To find Him, the greatest human achievement.*

RAPHAEL SIMON

The one universal element which pervades all experience is the emergence of a new life, with standards and values of its own, involving a progressive discipline, in which the self-principle is slowly put to death, and God becomes the center of the whole life.

EMILY HERMAN
Creative Prayer

Something has happened in the stillness that makes the person more tender, more sensitive, more shocked by evil, more dedicated to ideals of life, and more eager to push back the skirts of darkness and to widen the area of light and love.

RUFUS M. JONES
New Eyes for the Invisibles

But those who hope in the LORD
will renew their strength.
They will soar on wings like eagles;
they will run and not grow weary,
they will walk and not be faint.

ISAIAH 40:31

Those who are so fortunate as to experience in one of its many forms the crisis which is called "conversion" are seized, as it seems to them, by some power stronger than themselves and turned perforce in the right direction. They find that this irresistible power has cleansed the windows of their homely coat of grime; and they look out, literally, upon a new heaven and a new earth.

EVELYN UNDERHILL
Practical Mysticism

Blessed is the man who trusts in the LORD,
whose confidence is in him.
He will be like a tree planted by the water
that sends out its roots by the stream.
It does not fear when heat comes;
its leaves are always green.
It has no worries in a year of drought
and never fails to bear fruit."

JEREMIAH 17:7–8

O what a wonderful, wonderful day—
Day I will never forget;

After I'd wandered in darkness away,
Jesus my Savior I met.
O what a tender compassionate friend—
He met the need of my heart;
Shadows dispelling,
With joy I am telling,
He made the darkness depart!

Heaven came down and glory filled my soul.
When at the cross the Savior made me whole;
My sins were washed away—
And my night was turned to day
Heaven came down and glory filled my soul!

JOHN W. PETERSON

In what way. . .God changes a soul
from evil to good—how He impregnates
the barren rock with priceless gems and gold—is,
to the human mind, an impenetrable mystery.

SAMUEL TAYLOR COLERIDGE

Important as is the moment of commitment, when deep and total consent is given, it cannot be overemphasized that a new process has been initiated in the life. The commitment itself releases vast creative energies, but these energies must be geared to the specific demands of the new life.

The transformation may be so gradual that it passes unnoticed until, one day, everything is seen as different. Somewhere along the road a turn has been taken, a turn so simply a part of the landscape that it did not seem like a change in direction at all. A person will notice that some things that used to be difficult are now easier; some that seemed all right are no longer possible. There has been a slow invasion of the Spirit of God that marked no place or time.   HOWARD THURMAN
Disciplines of the Spirit

The experience of religion remains unchanged. That experience through the ages has been that through religion it is possible to lay hold on power for living which life without religion does not possess.   HENRY P. VAN DUSEN
Life's Meaning:
The Way and How of Christian Living

Just as soon as we turn toward Him with loving confidence, and say, "Thy will be done," whatever chills or cripples or enslaves our spirits, clogs their powers, or hinders their development, melts away in the sunshine of His sympathy. He does not free us from the pain, but from its power to dull the sensibilities; . . .not from disappointment, but from the hopelessness and bitterness of thought which it so often engenders. We attain unto this perfect liberty when we rise superior to untoward circumstances, triumph over the pain and weakness of disease, over unjust criticism, the wreck of earthly hopes, over promptings to envy, every sordid and selfish desire, every unhallowed longing, every doubt of God's wisdom and love and kindly care, when we rise into an atmosphere of undaunted moral courage, of restful content, of childlike trust, of holy, all-conquering calm.   WILLIAM W. KINSLEY

Because of your new sensitiveness,
anthems will be heard of you from every gutter,
poems of intolerable loveliness
will bud from every weed.
Best and greatest, your fellowmen will shine
with new significance and light.

EVELYN UNDERHILL

The power within is a strangely energizing power; it literally quickens the senses and also it quickens the apprehension, sharpening perception with appreciation. The humdrum in daily life begins to stir with meaning. Such deadening activities as have no place in our new way of life begin to slough off; they just don't belong and they can't adhere. Once we are alert to God's gifts we find ourselves looking expectantly into each new set of circumstances. MARGUERITE HARMON BRO
More Than We Are

If anyone is in Christ, he is a new creation;
the old has gone, the new has come!

2 CORINTHIANS 5:17

And whoever saith that
he hath had enough of it,
and may now lay it aside,
hath never tasted nor known it;
for he who hath truly felt or tasted it
can never give it up again.

THEOLOGIA GERMANICA

I come to the garden alone,
While the dew is still on the roses,
And the voice I hear, falling on my ear,
The Son of God discloses.

And He walks with me, and He talks with me,
And He tells me I am His own,
And the joy we share as we tarry there,
None other has ever known.

He speaks, and the sound of His voice
Is so sweet the birds hush their singing!
And the melody that He gave to me
Within my heart is ringing.

C. AUSTIN MILES

Let us give ourselves to God without any reserve, and let us fear nothing. He will love us, and take the place of everything else for us. He will fill our whole hearts; He will deprive us only of those things that make us unhappy. He will cause us to do in general, what we have been doing already, but which we have done in an unsatisfactory manner; whereas, hereafter, we shall do them well, because they will be done for His sake. Even the smallest actions of a simple and common life will be turned into consolation and recompense. We shall meet the approach of death in peace; it will be changed for us into the beginning of the immortal life.

FRANCOIS FENELON

Wherever there has been a faithful following of the Lord in a consecrated soul, several things have sooner or later followed. Meekness and quietness; a submissive acceptance of the will of God; pliability in the hands of God; sweetness under provocation, calmness in the midst of turmoil and bustle; a yielding to the wishes of others and an insensibility to slights and affronts; absence of worry or anxiety; deliverance from care and fear. God's glory and the welfare of His creatures become the absorbing delight of the soul.   HANNAH WHITALL SMITH
The Christian's Secret of a Happy Life

We, like the psalmist, are pilgrims in a land not our own. For if we have found God—or rather, have been found of Him—then we can never again really be at home in this world. Often, amid all the trafficking, and low thought of irreverent and godless men, we too will feel the high pull of the mountains and yearn for the pure air of the sunbathed peaks of God. And no man, caught in the smoke and miasma of the world's flat plains, ever need feel ashamed at this call of the hills. It is but the sign and seal that he is yet spiritually alive.

THOMAS H. NEWCOMB

Did you once drink at this fountain of living waters, you would not seek elsewhere for anything to quench your thirst; for while you still continue to draw from this source, you would thirst no longer after the world. MARIE GUYON
Autobiography

THE RELIGIOUS EXPERIENCE IS UNEXPLAINABLE AND INCOMPREHENSIBLE

At the heart of religious experience there is a paradox. Men of spiritual insight are, in the depths of their souls, conscious of a Presence, which they call God, and this Presence is more real to them than anything else that they know. They are not, however, about to describe it as other things can be described nor do they know it as they know other things. They are compelled to say that, in terms of the human intellect, God, since He cannot be comprehended by the rational faculty, is unknown and unknowable. That, however, is only half the picture. Though unknown and unknowable by the intellect, by what Dionysius the Areopagite calls the "higher faculty," it is possible for a man to be united "to Him Who is wholly unknowable, thus by knowing nothing he knows That Which is beyond knowledge."

JOHN OF THE CROSS
The Ascent of Mount Carmel

DRUID KING OF THE PICTS: "What difference will it make if I become Christ's man?"
BRENDAN, A CELTIC MONK: "If you become Christ's man, you will behold wonder on wonder, and every wonder true."

ANCIENT SCOTTISH ANNALS

Christ said, "I am come that ye might have life." Life is back of love, back of believing, back of hoping, back of everything. Ezekiel in his vision of the "River of Life" understood life; he knew what it meant—at first a little stream to the ankles, then, as he went further on, it came to the knees, and then to the loins, and finally a wide mighty river. That is life. Do you know what life is? No, neither does anybody else. Life is indefinable; life is an ultimate; life is God; life is effectiveness; life is power. Adjustment to the things around you—correspondence to environment—that is life. The plodding man does not live. He goes out of the spring, sweetly singing in the trees. The flowers are blooming in the fields, the whole sweet primrose growing on the bank does not for him contain life and beauty and music—it remains a primrose still. Life is measured by the number of things you are alive to. The fullness of our life means what we are about to do. I must have a life that is more abundant than my own poor nature. I must take the power of Jesus and have inside fellowship with Him.

MALTBIE D. BABCOCK
Thoughts for Every-day Living

Now, it may be asked, what is the state of a man who followeth the true Light to the utmost of his power? I answer truly, it will never be declared aright, for he who is not such a man, can neither understand nor know it, and he who is, knoweth it indeed; but he cannot utter it, for it is unspeakable. Therefore let him who would know it, give his whole diligence that he may enter therein; then will he see and find what hath never been uttered by man's lips.   THEOLOGIA GERMANICA

CLOSING PRAYER

Dear heavenly Father,
thank You for allowing us to find You.
Finding this "pearl of great price"
has made all the difference.
There is no turning back for we have tasted
Your sweet nectar and desire more.
Amen.

CHAPTER 9

We Walk by Faith,
Not by Sight

*"If anyone is thirsty, let him come to me and drink.
Whoever believes in me, as the Scripture has said,
streams of living water will flow from within him."*

John 7:37–38

Faith is the gift of God and God will give it to those who ask for it. You cannot argue or coax or reason or intellectualize and get faith. It is not something you learn. Your teacher is simply a spiritual farmer who prepares the soil for the seed which God drops into the fertile soil. Faith in God enlarges our perspective. It gives us an awareness that there is more to life than the basic material one. There is an invisible, but real life which infuses us with an indescribable peace of mind. One reason why more people do not receive this gift is because of pride. How can we know God if we think we already know everything and are filled with ourselves? "For it is by grace you have been saved, through faith—and this not from yourselves, it is the gift of God—not by works, so that no one can boast" (Ephesians 2:8–9).

FAITH IS THE GIFT OF GOD TO US

Oh how glorious our Faith is!
Instead of restricting hearts,
as the world fancies,
it uplifts them and enlarges their capacity to love.

THERESE OF LISIEUX

Though you have not seen him, you love him;
and even though you do not see him now,
you believe in him and are filled with
an inexpressible and glorious joy.

1 PETER 1:8

If we believe that everything is illuminated and takes shape around us: Chance is seen to be order, success assumes an incorruptible plenitude, suffering becomes a visit and a caress of God. But if we hesitate, the rock remains dry, the sky dark, the waters treacherous and shifting.

PIERRE TEILHARD DE CHARDIN

Faith is a voluntary anticipation.

CLEMENT OF ALEXANDRIA
Stromateis

Religious faith, when it comes to its true power, does just that miraculous thing for us all. It turns water to wine. It brings prodigals home. It sets men on their feet. It raises life out of death. It turns sunsets to sunrises. It makes the impossible become possible. The master secret of life is the attainment of the power of serenity in the midst of stress and action and adventure.

RUFUS M. JONES
New Eyes for Invisibles

Understanding is the reward of faith,
therefore seek not to understand that you may believe,
but believe that you may understand.

AUGUSTINE OF HIPPO
St. Julius Gospel

Faith is a work of God in us which changes us and brings us a new life from God. It makes us completely different people in heart, mind, senses, and all our powers, and brings the Holy Spirit with it. What a living, creative, active, powerful thing is faith! Faith is a living, unshakable confidence in God's grace. Through faith, a person will do good to every one without coercion, willingly and happily; he will serve everyone, suffer everything for the love and praise of God, who has shown him such grace. It is as impossible to separate works from faith as it is to separate heat and light from fire.

MARTIN LUTHER
Preface of the Letter of St. Paul to the Romans

A man cannot have faith without asking,
neither can he ask it without faith.

EDWARD MARBURY

Christian faith is a grand cathedral, with divinely pictured windows,—standing without, you can see no glory, nor can imagine any, but standing within every ray of light reveals a harmony of unspeakable splendors.   NATHANIEL HAWTHORNE

*To believe in God is to know
that all the rules will
be fair and that there will
be wonderful surprises.*

UGO BETTI

Both Scripture and tradition reveal to us that our very existence has its origin, foundation, and fulfillment in a divine call to share in God's life. Our faith is our personal awakening and response to this call. The deeper our faith the more keenly is felt the need to give ourselves entirely to God, who gave Himself entirely to us in creating us moment by moment in His image and likeness for Himself alone. Our faith awakens in us the awareness of God's self-giving love and thus sets in motion a reciprocity of love in moving us to give ourselves to God with all the loving abandon in which He gives Himself to us.   JAMES FINLEY
The Awakening Call

My soul finds rest in God alone;
my salvation comes from him.

PSALM 62:1

The kingdom of heaven is faith, when it dwells and reigns in the heart. Blessed are the eyes that see this kingdom; flesh and blood have not seen it; earthly wisdom is blind to it. To realize its glories, we must be born again, and to do this we must die to self.

FRANCOIS FENELON
Writings

Taste and see that the LORD is good;
blessed is the man who takes refuge in him.

PSALM 34:8

Trust God for great things;
with your five loaves and two fishes,
He will show you a way to feed thousands.

HORACE BUSHNELL

*Nothing that is not God
can fulfill my expectation.*

BLAISE PASCAL
Pensées

WE DEDICATE OURSELVES TO GOD

Give me, O Lord, a steadfast heart,
    which no unworthy affection may drag
    downwards;
Give me an unconquered heart,
    which no tribulation can wear out;
Give me an upright heart,
    which no unworthy purpose may tempt aside.
Bestow on me also, O Lord my God,
    understanding to know You, diligence to
    seek You, wisdom to find You, and a
    faithfulness that may finally embrace You,
    through Jesus Christ our Lord. Amen.

THOMAS AQUINAS

It's not the possession of extraordinary gifts
that makes extraordinary usefulness,
but the dedication of what we have
to the service of God.

FREDERICK W. ROBERTSON

Behold, Lord, an empty vessel that needs to be filled. My Lord, fill it. I am weak in the faith; strengthen me. I am cold in love; warm me and make me fervent, that my love may go out to my neighbor. I do not have a strong and firm faith; at times I doubt and am unable to trust You altogether. O Lord, help me. Strengthen my faith and trust in You. In You I have sealed the treasure of all I have. MARTIN LUTHER

He will cover you with his feathers,
and under his wings you will find refuge;
his faithfulness will be your shield and rampart.

PSALM 91:4

The great thing is to resign all your interests and pleasures and comfort and fame to God. He who unreservedly accepts whatever God may give him in this world—humiliation, trouble, and trial from within or from without—has made a great step towards self-victory; he will not dread praise or censure, he will not be sensitive; or if he finds himself wincing, he will deal so cavalierly with his sensitiveness that it will soon die away. Such full resignation and unfeigned acquiescence is true liberty, and hence arises perfect simplicity. Blessed indeed are they who are no longer their own, but have given themselves wholly to God!

FRANCOIS FENELON
Letters

The moment we make up our minds that we are going on with this determination to exalt God over all, we step out of the world's parade. We shall find ourselves out of adjustment to the ways of the world, and increasingly so as we make progression the holy way. We shall acquire a new viewpoint; a new and different psychology will be formed within us; a new power will begin to surprise us by its upsurgings and its outgoings.   A. W. TOZER
The Pursuit of God

They that wait upon the LORD shall renew their strength; they shall mount up with wings as eagles; they shall run, and not be weary; and they shall walk, and not faint." What, then are these wings? Their secret is contained in the words, "They that wait upon the LORD." The soul that waits upon the Lord is the soul that is entirely surrendered to Him, and that trusts Him perfectly. Therefore we might name our wings the wings of surrender and of trust. I mean by this, that if we will only surrender ourselves utterly to the Lord, and will trust Him perfectly, we shall find our souls "mounting up with wings as eagles" to the "heavenly places" in Christ Jesus, where earthly annoyances or sorrows have no power to disturb us.

The mother eagle teaches her little ones to fly by making their nest so uncomfortable that they are forced to leave it and commit themselves to the unknown world of air outside. And just so does our God to us. He stirs up our comfortable nests, and pushes us over the edge of them, and we are forced to use our wings to save ourselves from fatal falling. Read your trials in this light, and see if you cannot begin to get a glimpse of their meaning. Your wings are being developed.

HANNAH WHITALL SMITH
The Christian's Secret of a Happy Life

Slowly, through all the universe, that temple of God is being built. Wherever, in any world, a soul, by free-willed obedience, catches the fire of God's likeness, it is set into the growing walls, a living stone. When, in your hard fight, in your tiresome drudgery, or in your terrible temptation, you catch the purpose of your being, and give yourself to God, and so give Him the chance to give Himself to you, your life, a living stone, is taken up and set into that growing wall. . . . Wherever souls are being tried and ripened, in whatever common-place and homely ways;—there God is hewing out the pillars for His temple. Oh, if the stone can only have some vision of the temple of which it is to lie as part forever, what patience must fill it as it feels the glows of the hammer, and knows that success for it is simply to let itself be wrought into whatever shape the Master wills.

PHILLIPS BROOKS

Give up yourself to God without reserve;
in singleness of heart,
meeting everything that every day brings forth,
as something that comes from God.

WILLIAM LAW

Take, Lord, all my liberty, my memory,
my understanding, and my whole will.
You have given me all that I have, all that I am,
and I surrender all to Your divine will,
that You dispose of me.
Give me only Your love and Your grace.
With this I am rich enough, and I have no
more to ask.

IGNATIUS OF LOYOLA

Each soul has its own faculty; it can help in some way to make the world more cheerful and more beautiful. This it is which makes life worth living. If we are living only for ourselves, our own amusement, luxury, advancement, life is not worth living. But if we are living as coworkers with Christ, as fellow-helpers with God, as part of the noble army of martyrs who bear witness to the truth in all time, then our lives are full of interest.

JAMES FREEMAN CLARK

CLOSING PRAYER

Lord, I would trust Thee completely;
I want constantly to be aware of
Thy overshadowing presence and
to hear Thy speaking voice.
I long to live in restful sincerity of heart.
I want to live so full in the spirit that
all my thoughts may be as sweet incense
ascending to Thee and every act of my life
may be an act of worship.
And all this I confidently believe
Thou wilt grant me through the merits of
Jesus Christ Thy Son.
Amen.

A.W. TOZER
The Pursuit of God

CHAPTER 10

SPIRITUAL GROWTH
REQUIRES DILIGENCE

Grow in the grace and knowledge of our Lord
and Savior Jesus Christ.
To him be glory both now and forever!

2 PETER 3:18

There are four main things which must have a place in any full and healthy religious life. We require, first, the means of gaining and holding a right attitude; secondly, right spiritual food. Thirdly we need an education which shall help growth; training our spiritual powers to an ever greater expansion and efficiency. Fourthly we ought to have some definite spiritual work, and must see that we fit ourselves to do it.   EVELYN UNDERHILL

*Unless a tree has produced
blossoms in spring you will
vainly look for fruit in autumn.*

AUGUST W. HARE

Finding the kingdom of heaven involves an inner process of growth undertaken during our life's journey. It begins seemingly small and insignificant, but through a process of growth becomes a mighty power. "The kingdom of heaven is like a mustard seed, which a man took and planted in his field. Though it is the smallest of all your seeds, yet when it grows, it is the largest of garden plants and becomes a tree, so that the birds of the air come and perch in its branches" (Matthew 13:31–32).

"This kingdom of heaven is like yeast that a woman took and mixed into a large amount of flour until it worked all through the dough" (Matthew 13:33). Without yeast, the bread will not rise. The inner power will cause our lives to be fulfilled. This fulfillment involves a growth which, like the mustard seed, begins as something very small, but becomes great and, like yeast, comes to permeate our whole life. Our inner life grows and others will "find shelter in our branches."

C. M. M.

*To become Christlike is the only thing in the
whole world worth caring for,
the thing before which every ambition of man
is folly and all lower achievement vain.*

HENRY DRUMMOND

The aster has not wasted spring and summer because it has not blossomed. It has been all the time preparing for what is to follow, and in autumn it is the glory of the field, and only the frost lays it low. So there are many people who must live forty or fifty years, and have the crude sap of their natural dispositions changed and sweetened before the blossoming time can come; but their life has not been wasted.   HENRY WARD BEECHER
Life Thoughts

Each circumstance and event, tragic or happy, is attracted to us by what we have been and are, and in itself offers to us, by a right reaction to it, the opportunity of spiritual development.

RAYNOR C. JOHNSON
The Imprisoned Splendour

God will not let any of us stay where we are, and yet the growth and progress must be our own. We may delay it and hamper it, but we yet may dare to hope that through experiences we cannot imagine, through existences we cannot foresee, that little seed may grow into a branching tree, and fill the garden with shade and fragrance.

But if we are indeed desirous to do better, to grow in grace, and yet feel ourselves terribly weak and light-minded, what practical steps can we take to the goal that we see far off? The one thing that we can do in moments of insight is to undertake some little responsibility which we shall be ashamed to discard. We can look round our circle, and it will be strange if we cannot find at least one person whom we can help; and the best part of assuming such a responsibility is that it tends to grow and ramify; but in any case there is surely one person whom we can relieve, or encourage, or listen to, or make happier.

ARTHUR CHRISTOPHER BENSON
The Silent Isle

*The joy of all mysteries is the certainty which
comes from their contemplation,
that there are many doors yet for the soul to open
on her upward and inward way.*

ARTHUR CHRISTOPHER BENSON
From a College Window

Have a teachable spirit of faith, and do not pay any attention to self. Simply trust everything into the hands of God, be humble, and open up to His grace. Through meditation and prayer, you will receive peace, and everything will gradually be worked out for you. And the things which, in your hour of temptation, seemed so difficult will disappear almost imperceptibly.   FRANCOIS FENELON
Spiritual Letters

AS OUR SPIRITUAL LIVES ARE ENHANCED, SO ARE ALL OTHER ASPECTS OF OUR LIVES

What we all need is to "consider the lilies of the field" and learn their secret. Grow, by all means; but grow in God's ways, which is the only effectual way. See to it that you are planted in grace, and then let the divine Husbandman cultivate you in His own way and by His own means. Put yourself out in the sunshine of His presence, and let the dew of heaven come down upon you, and see what will be the result. Leaves, flowers, and fruit must surely come in their season. Only see to it that you oppose no hindrance to the shining of the Sun of Righteousness, or the falling of the dew from heaven. The thinnest covering may serve to keep off the sunshine and the dew, and the plant may wither, even where these are the most abundant. And so also the slightest barrier between your soul and God may cause you to dwindle and fade, as a plant in a cellar.

Keep the sky clear. Open wide every avenue of your being to receive the blessings your God may bring to bear upon you. Bask in the sunshine of His love. Drink the waters of His goodness. Keep your face upturned to Him, as the flowers do the sun. Look, and your souls shall live and grow.

To grow as do the lilies means an interior abandonment of the rarest kind. We are to be infinitely passive regarding ourselves, but infinitely active with regard to our attention and response to God. Self must step aside to let God do the work. Maybe you feel yourself planted in a desert soil where nothing can grow. Even so, trust fully in God, the divine Husbandman. He will make the very desert blossom as the rose and you "shall be as a tree planted by the waters. . .and shall not see when heat cometh. . .neither shall cease from yielding fruit."　　HANNAH WHITALL SMITH

The Christian's Secret of a Happy Life

Life is a building. It rises slowly, day by day throughout the years. Every new lesson we learn lays a block on the edifice, which is rising silently within us. Every experience, every touch of another life on ours, every influence that impresses us, every book we read, every conversation we hear, every act of our commonest days, adds something to the invisible building.   JAMES R. MILLER

Whatever you do, whether in word or deed,
do it all in the name of the Lord Jesus,
giving thanks to God the Father through him.

COLOSSIANS 3:17

As we grow in the spirit of the Lord we find grand vistas opening up all around with God's presence felt in all corners. Our life becomes a glorious acknowledgment of His power and mercy, and each step we take, we take in reverence and awe.

C. M. M.

I have four things to learn in life:
To think clearly without hurry or confusion;
To love everybody sincerely;
To act in everything with the highest motives;
To trust in God unhesitatingly.

HELEN KELLER

Let our temper be under the rule of the love of Jesus: He can not alone curb it,—He can make us gentle and patient. Let the vow, that not an unkind word of others shall ever be heard from our lips, be laid trustingly at His feet. Let the gentleness that refuses to take offense, that is always ready to excuse, to think and hope the best, mark our intercourse with all. Let our life be one of self-sacrifice, always studying the welfare of others, finding our highest joy in blessing others.

ANDREW MURRAY

Little self-denials, little passing words of sympathy,
little nameless acts of kindness,
little silent victories over favorite temptations—
these are the silent threads of gold which,
when woven together,
gleam out so brightly in the pattern of life
that God approves.

FREDERICK W. FARRAR

CLOSING PRAYER

Grant me, O Lord,
to know what is worth knowing and to love what is
worth loving.
Do not let me judge by what I see,
nor pass sentence according to what I hear,
but to judge rightly between things that differ,
and above all to search out
and to do what pleases You,
through Jesus Christ our Lord.

THOMAS À KEMPIS
The Imitation of Christ

PART FOUR

The Joyful Soul—
After Finding the
Pearl of Great Price

*"Peace I leave with you; my peace I give you.
I do not give to you as the world gives."*

John 14:27

*He who wants to be the friend of Christ must
    forsake much that the world counts friendship;
he who desires to see God must close his eyes to
    many things which the world thinks desirable;
and he who wishes to hear the voice of the Spirit
    must stop his ears against the babble of tongues
and put a seal upon his lips.*

Emily Herman

CHAPTER 11

IN GOD'S PRESENCE
IS FULLNESS OF JOY

"You have made known to me the path of life;
you will fill me with joy in your presence,
with eternal pleasures at your right hand."

PSALM 16:11

Joy is not something we can achieve by pursuing it. It is rather something born in the heart of the one who has found companionship with God and which overflows into a life in harmony with God. Regardless of outer circumstances, wealth or poverty, health or sickness, it visits the souls of those who are committed in their journey with Him. If we look upon all as under God's influence, life will become increasingly full of joy, which no one can take from us. No life can be dull when there is always that watchful expectancy, that anticipation of glad surprise and wonder of how God is using those seemingly little incidents in our lives to His glory and honor. Happiness is a very elusive thing. Yet it can be found in the simplest places. It is always knocking on our door, but we do not recognize it. It is not free, yet we cannot buy it. It comes on birds' wings as we go about our lives serving our Master in the way He has planned for each one of us.

INDESCRIBABLE JOY WILL BE OURS

Let us walk joyfully over this earth answering to that of God in every man.

GEORGE FOX

Joy is more divine than sorrow, for joy is bread and sorrow is medicine.

HENRY WARD BEECHER
Life Thoughts

Joy is distinctly a Christian word and Christian thing. It is the reverse of happiness. Happiness is the result of what happens of an agreeable sort. Joy has its springs deep down inside. And that spring never runs dry, no matter what happens. Only Jesus gives that joy. He had joy, singing its music within, even under the shadow of the cross. It is an unknown word and thing except as He has sway within.   SAMUEL DICKEY GORDON

Joy will be ours in so far as we are genuinely interested in great ideas outside ourselves. When we have once crossed the charmed circle and got outside ourselves, we shall soon realize that all true joy has an eternal and Divine source and goal. We are immortal spirits, set to do certain things in time; were it not so, our lives would lack any rational justification. The joy of achievement is the recognition of a task understood and done. It is done, and fit to take its place—however lowly a place—in the eternal order. . . . To do our duty in our own sphere, to try to create something worth creating, as our life's work, is the way to understand what joy is in this life, and by God's grace to earn the verdict: "Well done, good and faithful servant; enter thou into the joy of thy Lord."   W. R. INGE
Personal Religion and the Life of Devotion

Joy is the echo of God's life within us.

JOSEPH MARMION
Orthodoxy

As soon as we discover a new insight into our faith, we are transported with joy, like a miser who has found a treasure. The true Christian, whatever the misfortunes which Providence heaps upon him, wants whatever comes, and does not wish for anything which he does not have. The more he loves God, the more he is content. The highest perfection, instead of overloading him, makes his yoke lighter.

FRANCOIS FENELON
Instructions

Seize thou the joy of every day,
For gladness thrills the common sod,
And every brook and every bird
May sing to you the joy of God!

RALPH S. CUSHMAN
Spiritual Hilltops

Joy is the flag flying over the citadel of the soul
indicating that the King is in residence.

AUTHOR UNKNOWN

There are still others who find their joy deep in the heart of their religious experience. It is not related to, dependent upon or derived from, any circumstances or conditions in the midst of which they must live. It is a joy independent of all vicissitudes. There is a strange quality of awe in their joy, that is but a reflection of the deep calm water of the spirit out of which it comes. It is primarily a discovery of the soul, when God makes known His presence, where there are no words, no outward song, only the Divine Movement. This is the joy that the world cannot give. This is the joy that keeps watch against all the emissaries of sadness of mind and weariness of soul. This is the joy that comforts and is the companion, as we walk even through the valley of the shadow of death.   HOWARD THURMAN

Joy is the most infallible sign of
the presence of God.

LEON M. BLOY

*If the day and the night are such
that you greet them with joy,
and life emits a fragrance like flowers
and sweet-scented herbs—
that is your success.*

HENRY DAVID THOREAU

There is a strange elusive joy that comes into life at times. We may call it the satisfaction of making things or the joy of creation. It must come in very real measure to all real artists, who paint pictures, make statues, design buildings, write music or poetry, or fine prose. They have to pay for it by going through hours of agonizing fumbling, when things will not cease to be clouded and the spiritual something they are feeling will not come clear. And they pay for it, too, through long hours of dogged labor, and even then are seldom satisfied. They are creators and they experience birth pangs. Nonetheless, the joy they experience is due to the fact they are in tune with the Creator. The inspiration that started and sustained them came from Him. A. H. GRAY

I have told you this so that
my joy may be in you and
that your joy may be complete."

JOHN 15:11

You will go out in joy
and be led forth in peace;
the mountains and hills
will burst into song before you,
and all the trees of the field
will clap their hands."

ISAIAH 55:12

This is the secret of joy. We shall no longer strive
for our own way, but commit ourselves, easily and
simply to God's way, acquiese in His will and in so
doing find our peace.   EVELYN UNDERHILL

We are all strings in the concert of His joy.

JAKOB BOEHME

HAPPINESS COMES IN
ALIGNING OUR WILL WITH GOD'S WILL

Happiness is a butterfly,
which, when pursued,
is always beyond our grasp, but which,
if you will sit down quietly,
may alight upon you.

NATHANIEL HAWTHORNE

Whatever changes a godly man passes through, he is happy because God, who is unchangeable, is his chosen portion. If he meet with temporal losses, and be deprived of many of his temporal enjoyments, or of all of them; yet God, whom he prefers before all those things which he hath lost still remains, and cannot be lost. While he stays here in this changeable, troublesome world, yet he is happy, because his chosen portion, on which he builds, as his main foundation for happiness, is above the world and above all changes.

JONATHAN EDWARDS

The Beatitudes are the essence of the gospel message. They tell what happens to people who embrace Jesus' teachings. They sum up what happiness is and how it is obtained. They are so comprehensive that one could almost say that the rest of the Gospels simply elaborate upon them and show how they can be carried out in the daily lives of His followers.   C. M. M.

Happiness is neither within us only,
nor without us;
it is the union of ourselves with God.

BLAISE PASCAL
Pensees

Happiness is like manna; it is to be gathered in grains, and enjoyed every day. It will not keep; it cannot be accumulated; nor have we got to go out of ourselves or into remote places to gather it, since it is rained down from heaven, at our very doors.   TRYON EDWARDS

The world has its own idea of blessedness. Blessed is the man who is always right. Blessed is the man who is satisfied with himself. Blessed is the man who is strong. Blessed is the man who rules. Blessed is the man who is rich. Blessed is the man who is popular. Blessed is the man who enjoys life. These are the beatitudes of sight and of this present world.

It comes with a shock and opens a new realm of thought, that not one of these men entered Jesus' mind when He talked of blessedness. "Blessed," said Jesus, "is the man who thinks lowly of himself; who has passed through great trials; who gives in and endures; who longs for perfection; who carries a tender heart; who has a passion for holiness; who sweetens human life; who dares to be true to conscience." JOHN WATSON

The way to happiness: Keep your heart free from hate, your mind from worry. Live simply, expect little, give much. Fill your life with love. Scatter sunshine. Forget self, think of others. Do as you would be done by. Try this for a week and you will be surprised. H. C. MATTERN

Happiness is the greatest paradox in nature. It can grow in any soil, live under any conditions. It defies environment. The reason for this is that it does not come from without but from within. Whenever you see a person seeking happiness outside himself, you can be sure he has never yet found it.   FORMAN LINCICOME

Happiness is the legitimate fruitage of love and service. Set happiness before you as an end, no matter in what guise of wealth, or fame, or oblivion even, and you will not attain it—But renounce it and seek the pleasure of God, and that instant is the birth of your own.   ARTHUR S. HARDY

What happiness is, the Bible alone shows clearly and certainly, and points out the way that leads to the attainment of it.—"In Cicero and Plato, and other such writers," says Augustine, "I meet with many things acutely said, and things that excite a certain warmth of emotions, but in none of them do I find these words, 'Come unto me, all ye that labor, and are heavy laden, and I will give you rest.' "   SAMUEL TAYLOR COLERIDGE

CLOSING PRAYER

Grant me, O Lord,
the inward happiness and the serenity which come
from living close to You.
Renew in me daily the sense of joy
and let the Eternal Spirit of the Father
dwell in my soul and body,
filling every corner of my heart with light and grace,
so that I may bear witness to the Light,
giving You thanks always for all things.
Amen.

CHAPTER 12

IN QUIETNESS AND TRUST
IS YOUR STRENGTH

ISAIAH 30:15

"Be still, and know that I am God."

PSALM 46:10

God comes to us when there is silence within us. Have you ever gone out and sat by a lake or stream just as the stars were coming out, when all was calm and peaceful? Somehow a quietness had come over you and you knew that you were in the presence of the Lord. God gives us an irresistible desire for solitude. It allows us to come in touch with Him. We begin with a time and a place for God. We are freed from our slavery to the approval and gratitude of others and our need to see ourselves as important. After we meet God in the inner depths of our soul, we see the world with a new light. We can then enjoy our regular activities in their proper perspective. Silence will begin to speak loudly and we will not be able to ignore the voice of God calling to us. Activity and busyness often hide God's voice, and if we do not leave the hustle and bustle behind, we will have a difficult time hearing Him calling us along our life's journey

SOLITUDE IS ONE OF THE DEEPEST DISCIPLINES OF THE SPIRITUAL LIFE

When you have shut your doors
and darkened your room,
remember never to say that you are alone:
for you are not alone,
but God is within,
and your genius is within.

EPICTETUS
Discourses

We can cultivate an inner solitude and silence that sets us free from loneliness and fear. Loneliness is inner emptiness. Solitude is inner fulfillment. Solitude is not first a place but a state of mind and heart.

There is a solitude of the heart that can be maintained at all times. Crowds or the lack of them have little to do with this inward attentiveness. It is quite possible to be a desert hermit and never experience solitude. But if we possess inward solitude we will not fear being alone, for we know that we are not alone. Neither do we fear being with others, for they do not control us. In the midst of noise and confusion we are settled into a deep inner silence.

There is an old proverb to the effect that "the man who opens his mouth, closes his eyes!" The purpose of silence and solitude is to be able to see and hear. Control rather than no noise is the key to silence. Teresa of Avila

Be able to be alone. Lose not the advantage of solitude. . .but delight to be alone and single with Omnipresence. . . . Life is a pure flame, and we live by an invisible sun within us.

Sir Thomas Browne

A wise man is never less alone
than when he is alone.

JONATHAN SWIFT

*It takes solitude,
under the stars,
for us to be reminded of our eternal origin
and our far destiny.*

ARCHIBALD RUTLEDGE

We need not wings to go in search of Him,
but have only to find a place
where we can be alone—
and look upon Him present within us.

TERESA OF AVILA

*Let us be silent that we
may hear the whisper of God.*

RALPH WALDO EMERSON

Then a great and powerful wind tore the mountains apart and shattered the rocks before the LORD, but the LORD was not in the wind. After the wind there was an earthquake, but the LORD was not in the earthquake. After the earthquake came a fire, but the LORD was not in the fire. And after the fire came a gentle whisper.

1 KINGS 19:11–12

It is important that we get still to wait on God. And it is best that we get alone, preferably with our Bible outspread before us. Then if we will, we may draw near to God and begin to hear Him speak to us in our hearts. I think for the average person the progression will be something like this: First a sound as of a Presence walking in the garden. Then a voice, more intelligible, but still far from clear. Then the happy moment when the Spirit begins to illuminate the Scriptures, and that which had been only a sound, or at best, now becomes an intelligible word, warm and intimate and clear as the word of a dear friend. Then will come life and light, and best of all, ability to see and rest in and embrace Jesus Christ as Savior and Lord of all.

A. W. TOZER
The Pursuit of God

Unfortunately, in seeing ourselves as we truly are, not all that we see is beautiful and attractive. This is undoubtedly part of the reason we flee silence. We do not want to be confronted with our hypocrisy, our phoniness. We see how false and fragile is the false self we project. We have to go through this painful experience to come to our true self. It is a harrowing journey, a death to self—the false self—and no one wants to die. But it is the only path to life, to freedom, to peace, to true love. And it begins with silence. We cannot give ourselves in love if we do not know and possess ourselves. This is the great value of silence. It is the pathway to all we truly want.

M. BASIL PENNINGTON
A Place Apart

Lord, the Scripture says: "There is a time for silence and a time for speech." Saviour, teach me the silence of humility, the silence of wisdom, the silence of faith. Lord, teach me to silence my own heart that I may listen to the gentle movement of the Holy Spirit within me and sense the depths which are of God.   FRANKFURT PRAYER

Love silence, even in the mind; for thoughts are to that as words are to the body, troublesome: much speaking, as much thinking spends. True silence is the rest of the mind; and it is to the spirit what sleep is to the body, nourishment and refreshment.

WILLIAM PENN
Advice to His Children

*How rare it is to find a soul
quiet enough to hear God speak.*

FRANCOIS FENELON
Instructions

Silence is in truth the attribute of God, and those who seek Him from that side invariably learn that meditation is not the dream but the reality of life; not its illusion but its truth; not its weariness but its strength.   JAMES MARTINEAU

We need to find God,
and He cannot be found
in noise and restlessness.
God is the friend of silence.

MOTHER TERESA OF CALCUTTA

In this noisy, restless, bewildering age, there is a great need for quietness of spirit. Even in our communion with God we are so busy presenting our problems, asking for help, seeking relief that we leave no moments of silence to listen for God's answers.

By practice we can learn to submerge our spirits beneath the turbulent surface waves of life and reach that depth of our being where all is still, where no storms can reach us. Here only can we forget the material world and its demands upon us.

ALICE HEGAN RICE
My Pillow Book

Let thy soul walk slowly in thee,
As a saint in heaven unshod,
For to be alone with silence
Is to be alone with God.

SAMUEL MILLER HAGEMAN

The very best and utmost of attainment
in this life is to remain still
and let God act and speak in thee.

MEISTER ECKHART

Silence is listening with all our might to God. This is prayer at its best. We must learn to be still and listen. We get away from scandals and rumors and judgments and through the practice of silent communion we begin to know the power of prayer. In silence we can close our minds to what the world thinks is desirable. The babble of the world is drowned out so we can hear the voice of the Spirit. We must be faithful to the practice of silence and we will reap rich rewards. C. M. M.

Silence is a gift of God,
to let us speak more intimately with God.

VINCENT PALLOTTI

BUSYNESS AND HURRYING
HINDER OUR SERENITY

We keep running because we falsely think that fulfillment is always there, not here. We love noise and excitement because we have nothing inside. It distracts us and makes us forget our loneliness and helps us escape from ourselves.   C. M. M.

Rushing is a sign of weakness. Quiet abiding is a sign of strength. Go on along the highway of the Kingdom until all that comes, that touches your outward lives and circumstances, has no power to ruffle your spirit-calm. Make it a delight so to train yourselves. Storms may rage, difficulties press hard, but you will know no harm...safe, protected and guided.   A. J. RUSSELL
God at Eventide

Certainly, in our own little sphere it is not the most active people to whom we owe the most. Among the common people whom we know, it is not necessarily those who are busiest, not those who, meteor-like, are ever on the rush after some visible charge and work. It is the lives, like the stars, which simply pour down on us the calm light of their bright and faithful being, up to which we look and out of which we gather the deepest calm and courage.

Phillips Brooks

Sermons

Communion with God was never more needful than now. Feverish activity rules in all spheres of life. Christian effort is multiplied and systematized beyond all precedent; and all those things make fellowship with God hard to compass. We are so busy thinking, discussing, defending, inquiring, or preaching and teaching and working, that we have no time, and no leisure of heart for quiet contemplation, without which the exercise of the intellect upon Christ's truth will not feed, and busy activity in Christ's cause may starve the soul.

Alexander Maclaren

I will not hurry through this day!
Lord, I will listen by the way,
To humming bees and singing birds,
To speaking trees and friendly words;
And for the moments in between
Seek glimpses of Thy great Unseen.

I will not hurry through this day;
I will take time to think and pray;
I will look up into the sky,
Where fleecy clouds and swallows fly;
And somewhere in the day, maybe
I will catch a whisper, Lord, from Thee!

RALPH S. CUSHMAN

For all the wants which disturb life, which make us uneasy to ourselves, quarrelsome with others, and unthankful to God; which weary us in vain labors and foolish anxieties; which carry us from project to project, and from place to place in a poor pursuit of we know not what, are the wants which neither God, nor nature, nor reason has subjected us to, but are solely infused into us by pride, envy, ambition, and covetousness.   WILLIAM LAW
A Serious Call to a Devout and Holy Life

CLOSING PRAYER

Lord, teach me to listen.
The times are noisy and my ears are weary
with the thousand raucous sounds
which continuously assault them.
Give me the spirit of the boy Samuel
when he said to Thee,
"Speak, for Thy servant heareth."
Let me hear Thee speaking in my heart.
Let me get used to the sound of Thy voice,
that its tones may be familiar
when the sounds of earth die away
and the only sound will be
the music of Thy speaking voice.
Amen.

A. W. TOZER
The Pursuit of God

CHAPTER 13

WE MUST GIVE UP SELF IF WE
WISH TO DRAW NEAR TO GOD

*"If anyone would come after me,
he must deny himself and
take up his cross and follow me."*

MATTHEW 16:24

The absolute gift is the gift of oneself, such as Jesus practiced it. By forgetting ourselves, we find ourselves and are able to draw near to God. If we truly feel that by ourselves we are nothing—then there is room for God to come in and be everything. In exercising personal rights we are building up animosity and ill will which will ultimately cause greater loss than we had gained at the moment. When we rejoice to serve humbly, when we are content to be ill thought of, when we bear reproach and scorn gladly, then what can disturb the serenity of the soul? "Whoever loses his life for my sake will find it" (Matthew 10:39). Outer success turns out to be inner failure. Only by selling all can we buy the infinite treasure.

PRIDE LEADS TO SPIRITUAL BLINDNESS

The proud man is deaf and blind to the world; he does not see the world, but only himself reflected in all things.　　　　ALEXANDER YELCHANINOV
Diary

Do not expose others' weaknesses in order to make them feel less able than you. Neither should you think on your superior skill with any delight, or use it to set yourself above another person. Remember that what is most important to God is that we submit ourselves and all that we have to Him. This requires that we be willing to endure whatever His will brings us, to be content in whatever state we are in, and to be ready for every change.

JEREMY TAYLOR
The Rule and Exercises of Holy Living

*When pride comes, then comes disgrace,
but with humility comes wisdom.*

PROVERBS 11:2

God walks with the humble; He reveals Himself to the lowly; He gives understanding to the little ones; He discloses His meaning to pure minds, but hides His grace from the curious and proud.

THOMAS À KEMPIS
The Imitation of Christ

Pride ultimately leads to spiritual blindness. When we make ourselves the center of all our activities and thought we become hardened to the feelings and desires of others. We think we see clearly, but in actuality, this pride causes us to become blind to the needs of those around us and to God's plan for our lives. We do not see our own weakness, but have an inordinate confidence in our own strength and rightness. This hinders us in our walk of faith. If one is freed from self, he is untroubled by anxiety and does not feel hurried. He does not seek power or prestige. He has found his true life in God and nothing can ruffle him.   C. M. M.

It is better to have but little knowledge with humility and understanding, than great learning which might make you proud. For a man's merits are not to be estimated by his having many visions, or by his knowledge of the Bible, or by his being placed in a higher position; but by his being grounded in true humility, and by his seeking always, purely, and entirely, the honor of God.

Thomas à Kempis
The Imitation of Christ

Whoever exalts himself will be humbled, and whoever humbles himself will be exalted."

Matthew 23:12

The inferiority-complex is nothing but pride, the concentration of attention on one's self, egotism under a different form. Neither self-exaltation nor the sense of nonentity would ever trouble the minds of the humble and simple.

Alexander Yelchaninov
Diary

*The man who thinks he knows something does not
yet know as he ought to know.*

1 CORINTHIANS 8:2

For all the wants which disturb human life, which
make us uneasy to ourselves, quarrelsome with
others, and unthankful to God; which weary us in
vain labors and foolish anxieties; which carry us
from project to project, from place to place, in a
poor pursuit of we know not what, are the wants
which neither God, nor nature, nor reason, hath
subjected us to, but are solely infused into us by
pride, envy, ambition, and covetousness.

WILLIAM LAW
A Serious Call to a Devout and Holy Life

*Pride must die in you,
or nothing of Heaven can live in you.*

WILLIAM LAW

It is good to be reminded of the subtleties of pride. There is the pride of the private life—the moods which tempt us to think more highly of ourselves than we ought to think. Perhaps they are more than moods. It may well be that what was once a mood, or a temporary device to help one over a rough place in the private journey, has settled into an established pattern of thought and attitude. The peril in thinking more highly of one's self than one ought to think is the effect that it has on the ability to live effectively within one's limitations. It blinds the inner eye and dulls the judgment. It exposes the individual to frustration and futility. It breeds arrogance and conceit while undermining the gentle grace of humility. There is a kind of boastfulness in effort even though there is no word uttered. Very often the way in which a thing is done says more than a thousand words. Humility is not merely an attitude; it manifests itself also in the quality of the deed.

HOWARD THURMAN
The Inward Journey

LET US NOT LET EGO
GET IN THE WAY OF SERVING GOD

We may let go of self-seeking. In the eternal life there is not greed. One hears of neither "mine" nor "thine." All things are for all. As the waters fled away from Tantalus, so do the good things of life flee from the grasping and selfish spirit. The richest experiences of life never come to those who try to win them selfishly. If they do gain their desires, they find them as ashes to the taste. But all blessings are in the way of him who, forgetful of self, tries to be helpful to the world, and who spends his life in loving deeds.

ANNA R. BROWN LINDSAY
What Is Worth While?

A high and great virtue it is for a man to overcome himself; for he that overcometh himself shall overcome all his enemies, and attain to all good. And yet a greater virtue would it be if a man suffered himself to be overcome by all men; for he would be lord over all his enemies.

FRANCIS OF ASSISI
The Little Flowers of St. Francis of Assisi

The more a man gives up his heart to God, to his vocation, and to men, forgetful of himself and of that which belongs to him—the greater poise he will acquire, until he reaches peace, quiet, joy.

ALEXANDER YELCHANINOV
Diary

A man may give away all his goods, yet that is nothing; and if he do many deeds of penitence, yet that is a small thing; and though he understand all knowledge, yet that is afar off; and if he have zealous devotion, yet music is lacking unto him, yea, one thing which is the most necessary to him of all. What is it then? That having given up all things besides, he give up himself and go forth from himself utterly, and retain nothing of self-love; and having done all things which he knoweth to be his duty to do, that he feel that he hath done nothing.

THOMAS À KEMPIS
The Imitation of Christ

Do nothing out of selfish ambition or vain conceit, but in humility consider others better than yourselves. Each of you should look not only to your own interests, but also to the interests of others."

PHILIPPIANS 2:3–4

Make me a captive, Lord,
And then I shall be free:
Force me to render up my sword,
And I shall conqueror be.
I sink in life's alarms
When by myself I stand;
Imprison me within Thine arms,
And strong shall be my hand.

GEORGE MATHESON
Hymns of Worship

So long as we are full of self
we are shocked at the faults of others.
Let us think often of our own sin,
and we shall be lenient of the sins of others.

FRANCOIS FENELON

Nobody should seek his own good,
but the good of others.

1 CORINTHIANS 10:24

There are plenty to follow our Lord halfway, but not the other half. They will give up possessions, friends and honors, but it touches them too closely to disown themselves.   Meister Eckhart

If anyone wants to be first,
he must be the very last,
and the servant of all."

Mark 9:35

So long, as a man seeks his own will and his own highest good, because it is his, and for his sake, he will never find it: For so long as he does this, he is not seeking his own highest good, and how then should he find it? But whosoever seeks, loves, and pursues goodness, as goodness and for the sake of goodness, and makes that his end, he will find the highest good, for he seeks it aright, and they who seek it otherwise do err.

Theologia Germanica

Whoever will labor to get rid of self, to deny himself according to the instructions of Christ, strikes at once at the root of every evil, and finds the germ of every good.　　FRANCOIS FENELON

As long as our mind is stayed on our dear selves, we will never have peace. Some people think more of themselves than of all the rest of the world. It is self in the morning, self at noon, and self at night. It is self when they wake up, and self when they go to bed. They are all the time looking at themselves and thinking about themselves instead of "looking unto Jesus." Faith does not look within; it looks without. It is not what I think, or what I feel, or what I have done, but it is what Jesus Christ is and has done, that is the important thing for us to dwell upon.　　DWIGHT L. MOODY

If you want to be miserable, think much about yourself; about what you want, what you like, what respect people ought to pay you, and what people think of you.　　CHARLES KINGSLEY

A death blow is a life blow to some
Who, till they died, did not alive become;
Who, had they lived, had died, but when
They died, vitality begun.

EMILY DICKINSON

If I wish to write on a white tablet, then no matter how fine the matter already written on it, it will confuse me and prevent me from writing down my thoughts; so that, if I still wish to use the tablet, I must first erase all that is written on it. Similarly, if God is to write His message about the highest matters on my heart, everything of ourselves must first come out. God is then free to do His will on His own level when my heart is free.

MEISTER ECKHART
Sermons

TEACH ME, O LORD, TO WALK HUMBLY BEFORE YOU

If anyone thinks he is somebody when he is nothing, he deceives himself.　　　GALATIANS 6:3

*Lord, grant that I may seek rather
to comfort than to be comforted;
to understand than to be understood;
to love than to be loved;
For it is by forgetting self that one finds;
it is by forgiving that one is forgiven;
it is by dying that one awakes to eternal life.*

Teresa of Avila

I am sure that you understand that it is not enough to be merely separated from the world. For we can be separated and be quite proud about it. So we need to give considerable attention to becoming lowly. And I want you to see clearly the distinction between these two things. In separation, we renounce the other things of the world. But when we turn to the subject of lowliness and humility we are then dealing with the inner self. Every shadow of pride must be left behind. You cannot imagine how dangerous pride is—especially if it is that pride of wisdom and morality which seems so right and kind.   Francois Fenelon
Spiritual Letters

CLOSING PRAYER

Lord, let my life be orderly, regular, temperate;
let no pride or self-seeking,
no covetousness or revenge,
no little ends and low imaginations pollute
my spirit and unhallow my words and actions.
Let my body be a servant of my spirit and
both my body and spirit be servants of Jesus,
doing all things for Your glory here.
Amen.

JEREMY TAYLOR

CHAPTER 14

SIMPLICITY IS THE BEGINNING OF WISDOM

*As servants of God
we commend ourselves in every way:
. . .having nothing,
and yet possessing everything.*

2 CORINTHIANS 6:4, 10

As our lives become more God-filled, they become marked by simplicity. We need fewer acquaintances but more friends, fewer duties, but performed more faithfully, fewer books, but better ones. Doing away with the superfluous will help us attain a singleness of purpose. We will see the uselessness of religious busyness, running here and there to committee meetings which are often good, but may not be our calling. Conformity to others' ideas of serving God means little to us for our uppermost duty and interest is in pleasing God by finding and doing what He has called us to do. In doing so we are filled with a renewed spirit. We will experience a radiant joy in the simple things of everyday living, in doing the things that are part of our specific assignment by God, not by someone else. True simplicity is found in attaching ourselves to God. In Him we find everything we need.

Consider that wonderful world of life in which you are placed, and observe that its great rhythms of birth, growth, and death—all the things that really matter—are not in our control. That unhurried process will go forward in its stately beauty, little affected by your anxious fuss. Find out, then, where your treasure really is. Discern substance from accident. Don't confuse your meals with your life, and your clothes with your body. Don't lose your head over what perishes. Nearly everything does perish: So face the facts, don't rush after the transient and unreal. Maintain your soul in tranquil dependence on God; don't mistake what you possess for what you are. Accumulating things is useless. Both mental and material avarice are merely silly in view of the dread facts of life and death. The White Knight would have done better had he left his luggage at home. The simpler your house, the easier it will be to run. The fewer the things and the people you simply must have, "the nearer you will be to the ideal of happiness—as having nothing, to possess all."

EVELYN UNDERHILL
The House of the Soul

*The simplicity which is in Christ
is rarely found among us.
In its stead are programs, methods,
organizations, and a world of nervous activities
which occupy time and attention
but can never satisfy the longing of the heart.*

A. W. TOZER
The Pursuit of God

In order to arrive at having pleasure in
everything,
Desire to have pleasure in nothing.
In order to arrive at possessing everything,
Desire to possess nothing.
In order to arrive at knowing everything,
Desire to know nothing.
In order to arrive at that wherein thou has
pleasure
Thou must go by a way wherein thou has
no pleasure.

In this detachment the spiritual soul finds its quiet and response; since it covets nothing, nothing wearies it when it is lifted up, nothing oppresses it when it is cast down, because it is in the center of its humility; but, when it covets anything, at that very moment it becomes wearied.

JOHN OF THE CROSS
The Ascent of Mount Carmel

Go confidently in the direction of your dreams! As you simplify your life, the laws of the universe will be simpler; solitude will not be solitude, poverty will not be poverty, nor weakness weakness.

HENRY DAVID THOREAU

When one begins to practice simplicity, the ego is deprived of the very strategy by which it sustains itself. Nothing will deflate the ego more effectively than to be recognized for what it is. It lives by pretension. It dies when the mask is torn away and the stark reality is exposed to the gaze of others.

Simplicity also avails in braking the tyranny of things. Ostentation, artificiality, ornamentation, pretentious style, luxury—all require things. One requires few things to be one's self, one's age, and one's moral, intellectual, or spiritual stature. What one is does not depend upon what one has.

ALBERT E. DAY
Discipline and Discovery

*How many undervalue the power of simplicity!
But it is the real key to the heart.*

WILLIAM WORDSWORTH

He is nearest to God
who needs the fewest things.

SOCRATES

When we are truly in this interior simplicity our whole appearance is franker, more natural. This true simplicity. . .makes us conscious of a certain openness, gentleness, innocence, gaiety, and serenity. O, How amiable this simplicity is! Who will give it to me? I leave all for this. It is the pearl of the Gospel.   FRANCOIS FENELON

In faithfully following Christ, the Heart is weaned from the Desire of Riches, and we are led into a Life so plain and simple, that a little doth suffice, and thus the way openeth to deny ourselves, under all the tempting allurement of that Gain of Unrighteousness.   JOHN WOOLMAN
The Journal and Essays
of John Woolman

Man is lifted up above earthly things by two wings —simplicity and purity. Simplicity must be in the intention, purity in the affection. If you seek after nothing but the will of God and your neighbor's benefit, you shall enjoy interior liberty.

THOMAS À KEMPIS
The Imitation of Christ

Simplicity brings back the joys of Paradise. Not that we have pure pleasure without a moment's suffering, but when we are surrendered to God, we are not grasping for pleasure, and even our troubles are received with thanksgiving. This inner harmony, and this deliverance from fear and the tormenting desires of self, create a satisfaction in the soul which is above all the intoxicating joys of this world put together.   FRANCOIS FENELON
Spiritual Letters

*Nothing is more simple than greatness;
indeed to be simple is to be great.*

RALPH WALDO EMERSON

We cannot, by observing rules, make ourselves simple. All we can do is to show our desire to remove the hindrances in our Lord's way, to empty ourselves so that we may be filled with the simplicity which is in Christ Jesus.   BEDE FROST

Do you know the more I look into life, the more things it seems to me I can successfully lack—and continue to grow happier. How many kinds of food I do not need, or cooks to cook them, how much curious clothing or tailors to make it, how many books I have never read, and pictures that are not worthwhile! The farther I run, the more I feel like casting aside all such impediments—lest I fail to arrive at the far goal of my endeavor.

DAVID GRAYSON
Great Possessions

Only the simple are the free. All the rest are under the tyranny of the ambitious ego, its demand for recognition and for things, and the preoccupation with people. Hence, only the simple are free to direct their attention to God steadily, uninterruptedly, and to enter into conscious, vivid, and redemptive fellowship with God. No wonder Jesus said, "Except ye be converted, and become as little children, ye shall not enter into the kingdom of heaven" (Matthew 18:3 KJV).

ALBERT E. DAY
Discipline and Discovery

You were trying to be simple for the sake of being simple. I wonder if true simplicity is ever anything but a by-product. If we aim directly for it, it eludes us; but if we are on fire with some great interest that absorbs our lives to the uttermost, we forget ourselves into simplicity. Everything falls into simple lines around us, like a worn garment.

DAVID GRAYSON
Great Possessions

Whatever is true, whatever is noble,
whatever is right, whatever is pure,
whatever is lovely, whatever is admirable—
if anything is excellent or praiseworthy—
think about such things.

PHILIPPIANS 4:8

In character,
in manners, in style,
in all things the supreme excellence
is simplicity.

HENRY WADSWORTH LONGFELLOW

God has given you a simplicity and candor which doubtless pleases Him very much. It is on this foundation that He wants to build. He wants from you a simplicity which will be as much His wisdom as it is not your own. He wants you to be small in your own eyes, and yielding in His hands like a little child. It is this childlikeness, so contrary to the spirit of man, and so urged in the Gospel, which God wants to put in your heart despite the corruption which rules in the world. It is by His simplicity and this littleness that He wants to heal you of whatever remains of lofty and cynical wisdom.

FRANCOIS FENELON

We are not rich by what we possess but rather by what we can do without.

IMMANUEL KANT

A hard, materialized heart, like a wayside soul gives God no access. A heart that is shallow, like thin soil on stony ground, gives a quick response, but offers no sustenance to God's truth and therefore no harvest. A heart absorbed in many mundane concerns, like thorny ground, soon chokes the spiritual aspirations to death. Only the heart that is clean, simple, and cultivated, like a plowed, weeded field, can receive and nurture the truth of God and reap a harvest of godly character.

Albert E. Day
Discipline and Discovery

Closing Prayer

Strengthen me, O God,
  by the grace of Your Holy Spirit;
grant me to be strengthened with might
  in the inner self, and to put away from
my heart all useless anxiety and distress,
  and let me never be drawn
aside by various longings after anything
  whatever, whether
it be worthless or precious; but may I
  regard all things as passing away, and
myself as passing away with them.
  Amen.

Thomas à Kempis

PART FIVE

The Developing Soul— the Inward Journey, Growing in God's Grace

The living of the spiritual life
is not the decision of a moment;
it is the achievement of a lifetime,
enabled and empowered by the Holy Spirit.

Bernhard Christenson

CHAPTER 15

CHARACTER IS SHOWN IN THE LITTLE EVERYDAY THINGS

Whatever is true, whatever is noble,
whatever is right, whatever is pure,
whatever is lovely, whatever is admirable—
if anything is excellent or praiseworthy—
think about such things.

PHILIPPIANS 4:8

Great spiritual profit comes from doing little, unconscious deeds of kindness which are not sought, loving those who think ill of us, and giving to those who cannot give in return. Faithfulness in important and conspicuous things is common, but it is the faithfulness in the little, ordinary things which nobody notices that shows real character and love. All faith involves discipline. True discipline is an application of the principles set forth in God's Word to all aspects of our lives, and as a result, we enter into a life-giving fellowship with God. We must make it a rule to be one hundred percent honest in all we do. That means being honest with ourselves, too. Truth is, first of all, what we really are. To be, think, or want something because it makes a better impression or conforms to the opinions of others is not being true. To overlook something not quite right or to live in a way we don't approve is not being true. These principles are the building blocks for developing character.

THE LORD REQUIRES US TO ACT JUSTLY, TO LOVE MERCY, AND TO WALK HUMBLY

Good habits are not made on birthdays, nor Christian character at the New Year. The workshop of character is every-day life. The uneventful and commonplace hour is where the battle is lost or won. MALTBIE D. BABCOCK
Thoughts for Every-Day Living

Spiritual maturity begins when we realize that we are God's guests in this world. We are not house-holders, but pilgrims, not landlords, but tenants; not owners, but guests.   C. WILLARD FETTER

There is no more searching test of the human spirit than the way it behaves when fortune is adverse and it has to pass through a prolonged period of disap-pointing failures. Then comes the real proof of the man. Achievement, if a man has the ability, is a joy; but to take hard knocks and come up smiling, to have your mainsail blown away and then rig a sheet on the bowsprit and sail on—this is perhaps the deepest test of character.

HARRY EMERSON FOSDICK

A man may be outwardly successful all his life long, and die hollow and worthless as a puff-ball; and he may be externally defeated all his life long, and die in the royalty of a kingdom established within him. A man's true estate of power and riches is to be in himself; not in his dwelling, or position, or external relations, but in his own essential character.   HENRY WARD BEECHER
Life Thoughts

*The Christian home is the Master's workshop
where the processes of character molding
are silently, lovingly, faithfully,
and successfully carried on.*

LORD HUGHTO

Character is the product of daily, hourly actions, words and thoughts: daily forgiveness, unselfishness, kindnesses, sympathies, charities, sacrifices for the good of others, struggles against temptation, submissiveness under trial. It is these, like the blinding colors in a picture, or the blending notes of music, which constitute the man.

JOHN MACDUFF

*Talents are best nurtured in solitude;
character is best formed in
the stormy billows of the world.*

JOHANN WOLFGANG VON GOETHE

LORD, who may dwell in your sanctuary?
　　Who may live on your holy hill?
He whose walk is blameless and
　　who does what is righteous,
who speaks the truth from his heart
　　and has no slander on his tongue,
who does his neighbor no wrong and
　　casts no slur on his fellowman,
who despises a vile man but honors those
　　who fear the LORD,
who keeps his oath even when it hurts,
who lends his money without usury and
　　does not accept a bribe against the
　　innocent.
He who does these things will never be
　　shaken.

PSALM 15

Great works do not always lie in our way,
　　but every moment we may do
little ones excellently, that is, with great love.

FRANCIS DE SALES
Introduction to the Devout Life

We are spending time well when we are paying it out to God, to buy the things He means our lives to own, whether He is putting before us a duty to be done, a friend to be won, a small service to be rendered, a book to be written, a child to be consoled, or a house to be set in order. There is time enough given us to do all that God means us to do each day and to do it gloriously! How do we know that the interruption we snarl at is not the most blessed thing that has come to us in long days?

ANNA R. BROWN LINDSAY
What Is Worth While?

What Jesus Christ would say to us if He could speak to us in audible voice now would be something like this: Be a person. Be a real person. Stand on your own feet. Do not be pushed about by passing fads. Live by an inward light. Be true to an inward loyalty. If skepticism divides the church, vulgarity discolors social living, the profit motive makes industry often cruel, and nationalism blockades the way to peace, do not yes, yes the situation. Have a conscience of your own and when in private life the clamor of the public grow very loud, do grow quiet, quiet enough to hear the best and catch the rhythm of the inward drum.

HARRY EMERSON FOSDICK

THE LORD DELIGHTS IN THOSE
WHO ARE TRUTHFUL

We need truthfulness not merely to live in harmony with other human beings, but it is essential if we are to live with God in intimate fellowship. By truthfulness we undermine the ego whose tyranny deflects attention to an awareness of God. As the Bible insists, we become aware of God when we seek God with all our hearts. We cannot seek with all our hearts until our hearts are freed from dominant ego-concerns. Truthfulness is one way to help abolish such self-centeredness.

ALBERT E. DAY
Discipline and Discovery

*Be truthful in all things,
honest with an honesty that can be
challenged by the world,
and by the standards of God's Kingdom, too.*

A. J. RUSSELL
God at Eventide

Be just and fair in all you do. Always put yourself in your neighbor's place, and put him into yours, and then you will judge fairly. Sell as you would buy, and buy as you would sell, and your buying and selling will alike be honest. These little dishonesties seem unimportant, because we are not obliged to make restitution, and we have, after all, only taken that which we might demand according to the strict letter of the law; but, nevertheless, they are sins against right and charity, and are mere trickery, greatly needing correction—nor does anyone ever lose by being generous, noble-hearted and courteous. Be sure then often to examine your dealings with your neighbor, whether your heart is right towards him, as you would have his towards you, were things reversed—this is the true test of reason.

FRANCIS DE SALES
Introduction to the Devout Life

Let truth and plainness, therefore, be the only ornament of your language, and study nothing but how to think of all things as they deserve, to choose everything that is best, to live according to reason and order, and to act in every part of your life in conformity to the will of God.   WILLIAM LAW
A Serious Call to a Devout and Holy Life

God is truth. Pride, ambition, revenge, competition —these have no eternal values; they don't even last a lifetime. If everything we do has an honest purpose, with absolutely no selfish motives, that's the way of truth, which is the way of Jesus, which is God's way.

The short cut for discovering God's will. . . . Put everything we think, say, or do to the test of truth. Is it God's way—the way of wisdom, goodness, and love? Then it's the way of truth, and God will work with us.   ANONYMOUS
Journal of an Ordinary Pilgrim

The man of integrity walks securely,
but he who takes crooked paths will be found out.

PROVERBS 10:9

Truth is the beginning of every good thing, both in Heaven and on Earth; and he who would be blessed and happy should be from the first a partaker of the truth, for then he can be trusted.   PLATO

Integrity is a great and commendable virtue. A man of integrity is a true man, a bold man, and a steady man; he is to be trusted and relied upon. No bribes can corrupt him, no fear daunt him; his word is slow in coming, but sure. He shines brightest in the fire, and his friend hears of him most when he most needs him. His courage grows with danger, and conquers opposition by constancy. As he cannot be flattered or frightened into what he dislikes, so he hates flattery and temporizing in others. He runs with truth, and not with the times; with right and not with might.

WILLIAM PENN
Advice to His Children

SIMPLE GOODNESS IS A BEAUTIFUL THING

Goodness cannot be measured in any way. It is impossible to say who has done more good and who less. A widow who gives away her last farthing gives more than a rich man who gives thousands. It is also impossible to measure goodness by utility or inutility.

As an instance of how goodness must be shown, take the woman who pitied Jesus, and in her emotion poured upon Him many pounds' worth of costly oil. Judas said she had done foolishly, because many people might have been fed on the price. But Judas was a thief; he spoke untruth, and in talking of the worldly value of the oil, he did not consider the poor. Not utility, not value, comes into the question, but the necessity of always, every minute; loving others, and giving up to them one's own.

LEO TOLSTOY
The Complete Works of Leo Tolstoy

Some folk think they may scold, rail, hate, rob, and kill too, so it be but for God's sake. But nothing in us unlike Him can please Him.

WILLIAM PENN
Some Fruits of Solitude

Our lack of compassion, our ruthlessness towards other men, is an impenetrable curtain between ourselves and God. It is as if we had covered a plant with a black hood, and then complained that it died from deprivation of sunlight.

ALEXANDER YELCHANINOV
Diary

CLOSING PRAYER

*Lord, help me to do all things
with a good intention and always to please You.
Help me never to knowingly say
what is not strictly true
and to always remember that You are
the God of Truth. In Jesus' name, I pray.
Amen.*

CHAPTER 16

Let Us Faithfully Persist in Our Walk with the Lord

Perseverance must finish its work
so that you may be mature and complete,
not lacking anything.

James 1:4

We are not called to be successful; we are called to be faithful, faithful to our dreams which God has placed in our hearts. Simple tasks faithfully done and persisted in, like steady drops of water wearing away a stone, will wear away difficulties and bring their own rewards. Through all our difficulties of circumstance, health, opportunity, and even the temperamental personalities that we come daily into contact with, God reaches us and guides us to the destination He has planned for us. The events by which He shapes and disciplines us are often difficult, but our humble acceptance of everything ensures us of deeper communion with Him. Often we are willing to embark upon any adventure, do anything, but to wait patiently upon the Lord. We must be as those who run a race, stumble and fall, rise and press on to the goal, not looking back. Let us be faithful to the task He has given us.

WE ARE CALLED TO BE FAITHFUL

Stand firm. Let nothing move you.
Always give yourselves fully to the work of the Lord,
because you know that your labor
in the Lord is not in vain.

1 CORINTHIANS 15:58

Whatever you do,
work at it with all your heart,
as working for the Lord.

COLOSSIANS 3:23

Let God act, and let us be content to be faithful to the light of the present moment. It carries with it all that we need to prepare us for the light of the moment to follow. And this sequence of blessings, which connects one with another like the links of a chain, prepares us unconsciously for the further sacrifices which we have not even glimpsed.

FRANCOIS FENELON

I don't claim anything of the work. It is His work. I am like a little pencil in His hand. That is all. He does the thinking. He does the writing. The pencil has nothing to do with it. The pencil has only to be allowed to be used.

MOTHER TERESA

Let love and faithfulness never leave you;
bind them around your neck,
write them on the tablet of your heart.

PROVERBS 3:3

The soul is made for action, and cannot rest till it be employed. Idleness is its rust. Unless it will up and think and taste and see, all is in vain. Worlds of beauty and treasure and felicity may be round about it, and itself desolate. If therefore you would be happy, your life must be as full of operation as God of treasure. Your operation shall be treasure to Him, as His operation is delightful to you.

THOMAS TRAHERNE
Centuries of Meditation

It is well to remember that even in the holiest undertakings, what God requires of us is earnest willing labor, and the use of such means as we can command; but He does not require success of us: that depends solely upon Himself, and sometimes in His very love for us He refuses to crown our best intentions with success.

JEAN-NICOLAS GROU

My business is not to remain myself,
but to make the absolute best of what God made.

ROBERT BROWNING

Let us, then, be up and doing
With a heart for any fate;
Still achieving, still pursuing.
Learn to labor and to wait.

HENRY WADSWORTH LONGFELLOW

Be faithful, even to the point of death,
and I will give you the crown of life."

REVELATION 2:10

To pursue joy is to lose it. The only way to get it
is to follow steadily, the path of duty, without
thinking of joy, and then, like sheep, it comes most
surely, unsought.   ALEXANDER MACLAREN
                    A Rosary of Christian Graces

Does the road wind uphill all the way?
Yes, to the very end.
Will the journey take the whole long day?
From morn to night, my friend.

CHRISTINA ROSSETTI,
from "Uphill"

The everyday cares and duties, which men call drudgery, are the weights and counterpoints of the clock of time, giving its pendulum a true vibration, and its hands a regular motion; and when they cease to hang upon the wheels, the pendulum no longer swings, the hands no longer move, and the clock stands still.

HENRY WADSWORTH LONGFELLOW

Thine is the seed time:
God alone beholds the end of what is sown
Beyond our vision weak and dim
The harvest time is hid with Him.

JOHN GREENLEAF WHITTIER

Let us not become weary in doing good,
for at the proper time we will reap
a harvest if we do not give up.

GALATIANS 6:9

He Who Is Faithful Over
a Few Things Is a Lord of Cities

Great occasions for serving God come seldom, but little ones surround us daily; and our Lord Himself has told us that "He that is faithful in that which is least is faithful also in much."

FRANCIS DE SALES
Introduction to the Devout Life

To fill a little space because God wills it; to go on cheerfully with the petty round of little duties, little avocations; to accept unmurmuringly a low position; to be misunderstood, misrepresented, maligned, without complaint, to smile for the joys of others when the heart is aching; to banish all ambition, all pride, and all restlessness, in a single regard to our Savior's work; he who does this is a greater hero than he who for one hour storms a beach, or for one day rushes onward undaunted in the flaming front of a shot and shell. His works will follow him. He may be no hero to the world, but he is one of God's heroes. FREDERICK W. FABER
Treasure Thoughts

He who is faithful over a few things is a lord of cities." It does not matter whether you preach in Westminster Abbey, or teach a ragged class, so you be faithful. The faithfulness is all.

GEORGE MACDONALD

Not a prayer, not an act of faithfulness in your calling, not a self-denying or kind word or deed, done out of love for Himself; not a weariness or painfulness endured patiently, not a duty performed; not a temptation resisted; but it enlarges the whole soul for the endless capacity of the love of God.

EDWARD B. PUSEY

Great thoughts go best with common duties.
Whatever therefore may be your office
regard it as a fragment in
an immeasurable ministry of love.

BROOKE F. WESTCOTT

Nothing is small or great in God's sight; whatever He wills becomes great to us, however seemingly trifling. Once the voice of conscience tells us that He requires anything of us we have no right to measure its importance. On the other hand, whatever He would not have us do, however important we may think it, is as nought to us. How do you know what you may lose by neglecting this duty, which you think is trifling, or the blessing which its faithful performance may bring? Be sure that you will not be left without sufficient help when some weightier occasion arises. Give yourself to Him, trust Him, fix your eye upon Him, listen to His voice, and then go on bravely and cheerfully.   JEAN-NICOLAS GROU

It is the habit of making sacrifices in small things that enables us for making them in great, when it is asked of us. Temper, love of preeminence, bodily indulgence, the quick retort, the sharp irony,— in checking these let us find our cross and carry it. Or, when the moment comes for some really great service, the heart will be petrified for it, and the blinded eyes will not see the occasion of love.

ANTHONY W. THOROLD

The occupations of every day seem trifling; we may do them without thinking them as ordinary things, yet they are the scenes of our appointed lot—appointed by God for you and me. The ordering, the application of these ordinary occupations, is the appointment of the Divine purpose; it is for ourselves to carry them out. And secretly our character forms according as we handle them. . . . Nothing comes by pure accident, not even the interruptions in our busy day. And such as follow on to know God's will see in all events what may lead to good, and so trust grows into a habit, as habit grows by perpetual use, till every circumstance may be seen to be but a fresh manifestation of the will of God working itself out in us.

THOMAS T. CARTER

After waiting patiently,
Abraham received what was promised.

HEBREWS 6:15

There is no music in a "rest," but there's the making of music in it. And people are always missing that part of the life melody, always talking of perseverance and courage and fortitude; but

patience is the finest and worthiest part of fortitude, and the rarest too.   JOHN RUSKIN

*Let us only be patient and let God our Father
teach His own lesson in His own way.
Let us try to learn it well and learn it quickly,
but do not let us fancy that
He will ring the school bell and
send us to play before our lesson is learned.*

CHARLES KINGSLEY

Patience with ourselves is a duty for Christians
and the only real humility. For it means patience
with a growing creature whom God has taken in
hand and whose completion He will effect in His
own time and way.   EVELYN UNDERHILL

Have courage for the great sorrows of life and
patience for the small ones; and when you have
laboriously accomplished your daily tasks, go to
sleep in peace. God is awake.   VICTOR HUGO

Let us not judge God by an incomplete or unfinished scheme. Let us have patience till the end shall justify the path by which we came. In the braking down of eternity, we shall discover that God could not have brought us by another route which would have been as expeditious or a sage as the one by which we have come.   FREDERICK B. MEYER

There are years in South Africa when locusts swarm the land and eat the crops. They come in hordes, blocking out the sun. The crops are lost and a hard winter follows. The "years that the locusts eat" are feared and dreaded. But the year after the locusts, South Africa reaps its greatest crops, for the dead bodies of the locusts serve as fertilizer for the new seed. And the locust year is restored as great crops swell the land.

This is a parable of our life. There are seasons of deep distress and afflictions that sometimes eat all the usefulness of our lives away. Yet, the promise is that God will restore those locust years if we endure. We will reap if we faint not. Although now we do not know all the "why's," we can be assured our times are in His hands.   RON HEMBREE

Fruits of the Spirit

CLOSING PRAYER

O Lord, we put our hope and trust in You.
Renew our strength.
Help us to soar on wings like eagles;
To run and not grow weary,
To walk and not be faint.
Through Jesus Christ our Lord. Amen.

from ISAIAH 40:31

CHAPTER 17

It Is Good That We Sometimes Suffer So That We Can Learn to Put Our Trust in God, Not in Worldly Things

*We also rejoice in our sufferings,
because we know that suffering produces
perseverance; perseverance, character;
and character, hope.*

ROMANS 5:3

Difficulties come. Trials, misfortunes, failures, discouragement, adversity, and pain seem inevitable. Suffering is a part of life and is necessary so that we may learn to adapt our lives to the teaching God has given us, that we may realize our own weakness, develop obedience, perseverance, and fortitude, and soften our hearts and strengthen us in faith, hope, and virtue. As a butterfly struggles to escape its cocoon and in so doing becomes strong enough to fly, so God allows difficulties in our lives so we may break the cocoon of our earthly life and develop enough strength to fly with the wings of our spirit. We sometimes think that we need prosperity to find happiness, but isn't it the one who has suffered and gone through difficult times who can render the greatest service to his fellowman? Our real blessings often appear to us in the form of pain and disappointments, but if we have patience we shall see that they are a part of the darkness where rare and beautiful blessings bloom even though the sunshine is absent for a season. How God must love us to want such great things for us!

GOD TOUCHES OUR LIVES
THROUGH SUFFERING

Count each affliction,
whether light or grave,
God's messenger sent down to thee.

AUBREY THOMAS DE VERE
Sorrow

Sweet are the uses of adversity
Which, like the toad, ugly and venomous,
Wears yet a precious jewel in his head;
And this our life, exempt from public haunt
Finds tongues in trees, books in the running
  brooks
Sermons in stones and good in everything.

WILLIAM SHAKESPEARE

If it seems to you that you have not yet suffered any tribulations, rest assured that you have not yet begun to be a true servant of God, because the Apostle clearly states that all those who wish to live piously in Christ will suffer persecutions.

AUGUSTINE OF HIPPO

Because of my chains,
most of the brothers in the Lord have been
encouraged to speak the word of God
more courageously and fearlessly.

PHILIPPIANS 1:14

Christ did not come to do away with suffering,
He did not come to explain it.
He came to fill it with His presence.

PAUL CLAUDEL

Character cannot be developed in ease and quiet.
Only through experience of trial and suffering
can the soul be strengthened, vision cleared,
ambition inspired, and success achieved.

HELEN KELLER

God knoweth best what is needful for us, and all
that He does is for our good. If we knew how much
He loves us, we should be always ready to receive
equally, and with indifference, from His hand, the
sweet and bitter; all would please that came from
Him. The sorest afflictions never appear intolerable, but when we see them in a wrong light. When
we see them in the hand of God, our suffering loses
all its bitterness, and our mourning becomes all joy.

BROTHER LAWRENCE
The Practice of the Presence of God

Blessed is the man who perseveres under trial,
because when he has stood the test,
he will receive the crown of life that
God has promised to those who love him.

James 1:12

The eternal stars shine out
as soon as it is dark enough.

Thomas Carlyle

Many men owe the grandeur of their lives to their tremendous difficulties. A high character might be produced, I suppose, by continued prosperity, but it has very seldom been the case. Adversity, however it may appear to be our foe, is our true friend; and, after a little acquaintance with it, we receive it as a precious thing—the prophecy of a coming joy. Charles H. Spurgeon

I have refined you, though not as silver; I have tested you in the furnace of affliction. For my own sake, for my own sake, I do this." Isaiah 48:10–11

Stars may be seen from the bottom of a deep well,
when they cannot be discovered from
the top of a mountain,
so are many things learned in adversity
which the prosperous man dreams not of.

Charles H. Spurgeon

Affliction comes to us all not to make us sad, but sober; not to make us sorry, but wise; not to make us despondent, but by its darkness to refresh us, as the night refreshes the day; not to impoverish, but to enrich us, as the plough enriches the field; to multiply our joy, as the seed, by planting, is multiplied a thousand-fold.   Henry Ward Beecher
Life Thoughts

Suffering keeps the soul humble
and teaches patience.
It imparts true confidence, a clear conscience,
and constant loftiness of mind.
Suffering draws and forces us to God,
whether we like it or not.

Henry Suso
A Little Book of Eternal Wisdom

Affliction is a treasure, and scarce any man hath enough of it. No man hath affliction enough that is not matured, and ripened by it, and made fit for God by that affliction.

JOHN DONNE
Devotions upon
Emergent Occasions

As sure as God puts His children
into the furnace of affliction,
He will be with them in it.

CHARLES H. SPURGEON

Afflictions are but
the shadow of God's wings.

GEORGE MACDONALD

Never was there a man of deep piety, who has not been brought into extremities—who has not been put into fire—who has not been taught to say, "Though He slay me, yet will I trust in Him."

RICHARD CECIL

The swiftest steed to bear you to your goal is suffering; none shall ever taste eternal bliss but those who stand with Christ in depths of bitterness. Nothing is more gall-bitter than suffering, nothing so honey-sweet as to have suffered.   MEISTER ECKHART
Sermons

*Christ suffered for you, leaving you an example,
that you should follow in his steps.*

1 PETER 2:21

When the barn is full, man can live without God: When the purse is bursting with gold, we try to do without so much prayer. But once take our gourds away, and we want our God; once cleanse the idols out of the house, then we are compelled to honor Jehovah. "Out of the depths have I cried unto thee, O Lord." There is no cry so good as that which comes from the bottom of the mountains; no prayer half so hearty as that which comes up from the depths of the soul, through deep trials and afflictions. Hence they bring us to God, and we are happier; for nearness to God is happiness.

CHARLES H. SPURGEON

An iron is fashioned by fire and on an anvil,
so in the fire of suffering and
under the weight of trials,
our souls receive the form which
our Lord desires them to have.

MADELEINE SOPHIE BARET

Wherever souls are being tried and ripened,
in whatever commonplace and homely way,
there God is hewing out the pillars
for His temple.

PHILLIPS BROOKS

There is nothing more painful than suffering, and nothing more joyful than to have suffered. Suffering is a short pain and a long joy. Suffering gives to the sufferer pain here and joy hereafter. Suffering kills suffering. The noble soul blooms by suffering even as the beautiful rose by the fresh dews of May! Suffering makes a wise mind and an experienced man. A man who has not suffered, what does he know?

HENRY SUSO

A Little Book of Eternal Wisdom

In this world you will have trouble.
But take heart! I have overcome the world."

JOHN 16:33

Many a man has thought himself broken up,
when he has merely been made ready
for the sowing.

HUGH REDWOOD

In all things
God works for the good
of those who love him,
who have been called
according to his purpose.

ROMANS 8:28

When the time after that terrible disappointment has passed and the awful strain has successfully been borne, we can say, "In the year that King Uzziah died, I saw the Lord." In the year in which I sustained that awful family loss, I saw the Lord. In the year in which I underwent an experience in my professional life that almost smote me to death, I saw the Lord. WILLIAM C. POOLE

I have refined you,
though not as silver;
I have tested you in the furnace of affliction.
For my own sake,
for my own sake,
I do this.

ISAIAH 48:10-11

The things we call trials and adversities are really God's angels, though they seem terrible to us; and if we will only quiet our hearts and wait, we will find that they are messengers from heaven, and that they bring blessing to us from God. They have come to tell us of some new joy that is to be granted—some strange and sweet surprise of love waiting for us. JAMES R. MILLER

God has not destined us to be rich, diseaseless, and deathless, but has given us trials, in the form of poverty, disease, the death of our friends and of ourselves—for the very purpose of teaching us to center our lives not in wealth, health, and this temporary existence, but in serving Him. And He has given us foes not in order that we should desire their ruin, but that we should learn to overcome them by love. He has given us a law of such a nature that it is always well with us if we fulfill it. LEO TOLSTOY
Personal Letters

No dogma of religion is surer than this:
If one would be close to God he must suffer.
WALTER ELLIOTT
The Spiritual Life

Suffering was a curse from which man fled, now it becomes a purification of the soul, a sacred trial sent by Eternal Love, a divine dispensation meant to sanctify and ennoble us, an acceptable aid to faith, a strange initiation into happiness.

HENRI-FREDERIC AMIEL
Journal

Trials are medicines which our gracious and wise physician prescribes, because we need them; and He proportions the frequency and weight of them to what the case requires. Let us trust His skill and thank Him for His prescription.   JOHN NEWTON

It was good for me to be afflicted
so that I might learn your decrees.

PSALM 119:71

PROBLEMS AND DISAPPOINTMENTS ALSO CAN AID OUR SPIRITUAL PROGRESS

Every contradiction of our will, every little ailment, every petty disappointment, will, if we take it patiently, become a blessing. So, walking on earth, we may be in heaven. The ill-tempers of others, the slights and rudeness of the world, ill-health, the daily accidents with which God has mercifully strewed our paths, instead of ruffling or disturbing our peace, may cause His peace to be shed abroad in our hearts abundantly.

EDWARD B. PUSEY

*Difficulties are God's errands;
and when we are sent upon them,
we should esteem it as proof of God's confidence.*

Henry Ward Beecher

Why does God bring thunderclouds and disasters when we want green pastures and still waters? Bit by bit we find, behind the clouds, the Father's feet; behind the lightning, an abiding day that has no night; behind the thunder, "a still small voice" that comforts with a comfort that is unspeakable. The whole claim of the redemption of Jesus is that He can satisfy the last aching abyss of the human soul, not only hereafter, but here and now.

Oswald Chambers
In the Presence of His Majesty

Now for a little while you may have had to suffer grief in all kinds of trials. These have come so that your faith—of greater worth than gold, which perishes even though refined by fire—may be proved genuine and may result in praise, glory and honor when Jesus Christ is revealed.

1 Peter 1:6–7

*Troubles are often the tools
by which God fashions us for better things.*

HENRY WARD BEECHER

God will not permit any troubles
to come upon us,
unless He has a specific plan by which
great blessing can come out of the difficulty.

PETER MARSHALL
Mr. Jones, Meet the Master

*If things always went wrong,
no one could endure it; if they always went well,
everyone would become arrogant.*

BERNARD OF CLAIRVAUX
Letters

Though outwardly we are wasting away, yet inwardly we are being renewed day by day. For our light and momentary troubles are achieving for us an eternal glory that far outweighs them all.

2 CORINTHIANS 4:16–17

The tests of life are to make, not break us. Trouble may demolish a man's business but build up his character. The blow at the outward man may be the greatest blessing to the inner man. If God then puts or permits anything hard in our lives, be sure that the real peril, the real trouble, is that we shall lose if we flinch or rebel.

MALTBIE D. BABCOCK
Thoughts for Every-Day Living

In case of any difficulty remember that God, like a gymnastic trainer, has pitted you against a rough antagonist. For what end? That you may be an Olympic conqueror, and this cannot be without toil.

EPICTETUS
Discourses

Each of us may be sure that if God sends us on stony paths, He will provide us with strong shoes. He will not send us out on any journey for which He does not equip us well.

MEGIDDO MESSAGE

Temptations are necessary in order that we may learn not to trust in our own strength. When the violence of the temptation is extreme; when our strength is exhausted through long resistance; when we see no way of escape and nothing seems left to us but to surrender; then, seeing no hope in ourselves and having no further defense, we must throw ourselves into the arms of God. This is just the moment God has been waiting for, and never more than now shall we receive His help.

JEAN-NICOLAS GROU
Spiritual Maxims

God is faithful;
he will not let you be tempted
beyond what you can bear.

1 CORINTHIANS 10:13

Neither let mistakes and wrong directions—of which every man, in his studies and elsewhere, falls into many—discourage you. There is precious instruction to be got by finding that we are wrong.

THOMAS CARLYLE

Patience is necessary in this life because so much of life is fraught with adversity. No matter how hard we try, our lives will never be without strife and grief. Thus, we should not strive for a peace that is without temptation, or for a life that never feels adversity. Peace is not found by escaping temptations, but by being tried by them. We will have discovered peace when we have been tried and come through the trial of temptation.

THOMAS À KEMPIS
The Imitation of Christ

Do not be grieved at your situation or be discontented. Do not look at the difficulty of your condition, but instead, when the storm rages against you, look up to Him who can give you patience and can lift your head over it all and cause you to grow.

ISAAC PENINGTON
Letters on Spiritual Virtues

Do you have failed? You cannot fail.
You have not failed:
You have gained experience. Forward!

JOSE ESCRIVA

After we have placed ourselves entirely in God's hands with complete confidence in Him, we must not fear any adversity; for if some misfortune should befall us, God will know how to turn it to our good through ways which we do not know now but will know some day.   VINCENT DE PAUL

Every trial that we pass through is capable of being the seed of a noble character. Every temptation that we meet in the path of duty is another chance of filling our souls with the power of Heaven.

FREDERICK TEMPLE

CLOSING PRAYER

*Dear Lord, help me to see more clearly
that You love me when You allow problems
to come into my life.
There is still much I need to learn.
I am so glad You have a plan for my life
and allow difficulties to bring me to a clear vision
and a depth of understanding of Your Purposes.
Amen.*

CHAPTER 18

Sorrow Is Sent by God
Because of His Unspeakable Love
for Us and His Desire for Us
to Draw Closer to Him

*Weeping may remain for a night, but
rejoicing comes in the morning.*

Psalm 30:5

It is through sorrow that God teaches us to walk
by faith. We are here to learn and sorrow may be
necessary for certain lessons. You can always recognize those who have been through the fires of
sorrow and tough times because you know you can
go to them in your moment of trouble and find
that they have plenty of time for you. The beauty
and the grandeur of the stars in heaven are only to

be seen when set against the darkness of night; so sorrow often reveals to us our Father, whom the sunlight of prosperity hides. The "dark night of the soul" is an experience of spiritual desolation, loneliness, and despair which grips the soul of the one who, having seen the vision of God and has been lifted by it, finds the vision fade and the presence of God recede. God uses this time to draw us closer to Him.

Those Who Sow in Tears Will Reap with Songs of Joy

For one thing is certain, that the end is not yet; and that there is something done for the soul both by the morning brightness and the evening heaviness which can be effected in no other way. And in this spirit we may look back on our mistakes, sad as they were, and on our triumphs, which are sometimes sadder still, and know that they were not mere accidents and obstacles which might have been otherwise—they were rather the very stuff and essence of the soul showing through its enfolding garb.

Arthur Christopher Benson
The Silent Isle

Tears are often the telescope through which men see far into heaven.

HENRY WARD BEECHER
Life Thoughts

Accepting the doctrine of the Cross we see our suffering as part of a pattern, woven into the tapestry, not on a single thread, but inseparably with His, and dyed in the same dye.

The soul hardly ever realized it, but, whether man is a believer or not, his loneliness is really a homesickness for God. The sense of loss and emptiness does not derive from being away from God. Until he has found his permanent place in God he is bound to feel more or less lonely—out of place—in the world.

God sees to it that man is uprooted from time to time and parted from those he loves, so that in the sadness which follows he may remember that he is but a pilgrim and a stranger upon the earth and that it will be time enough later on to settle down and live happily ever afterwards. If our homesickness teaches us where to look for what we want, it will not have been suffered in vain.

HUBERT VAN ZELLER
We Die Standing Up

A tree has both straight and crooked branches; the symmetry of the tree, however, is perfect. Life is balanced like a tree. When you consider the struggles, difficulties, and sorrows as a part of it, then you see it beautiful and perfect.

GEORGE M. LAMSA
Gems of Wisdom

No Christian escapes a taste of the wilderness on the way to the Promised Land.

EVELYN UNDERHILL
The Fruits of the Spirit

*Cast your cares on the LORD
and he will sustain you.*

PSALM 55:22

Sorrows are often like clouds, which though black when they are passing over us, when they are past become as if they were the garments of God thrown off in purple and gold along the sky.

HENRY WARD BEECHER

When it is dull and cold and weary weather with us, when the light is hidden, and the mists are thick, and the sleet begins to fall, when we seem poorest and least spiritual, when the glow of thankfulness seems to have died quite away, through humbly and simply doing what we can, we retrieve the power of doing what we would. When you find yourself overpowered by melancholy, the best thing is to go out and do something kind to somebody or other.

FRANCIS PAGET
The Spirit of Discipline

A remedy against sadness is to break out of it by some external act of kindness or generosity. For the malady consists in a morbid concentration upon one's self, and a brooding within one's self that repels sympathy and kindness, as being adverse to this melancholy mood, a mood that can only be cherished in isolation of spirit. But let the will make a little effort to be kind and considerate towards another; and it is amazing how soon that malignant charm is broken that held the soul spellbound to her saddened thoughts and imaginary grievances. A smile, a kind look, a few gentle words, a considerate action, though begun with effort, will suffice to open the soul, and set the spirit free from its delusion.

WILLIAM B. ULLATHORNE

God is the divine Artist of our lives, which will not be completed until He adds the final touch of color, the last detail. We are God's canvas, and our task is simply to receive the colors He has designed for us—the darks and the lights, the somber and the bright. Some of the details may seem meaningless until the last colors are added, but someday we will see it all—our life painting completed by the Master Artist. Only then will we see the reason for the dark background—perhaps as a contrast to the final brilliant flourish of His brush as He completes His work and our lives culminate in His glorious presence.

AL BRYANT
Here's a Faith for You

It is the veiled angel of sorrow who plucks away one thing and another that bound us here in ease and security, and in vanishing of those dear objects, indicates the true home of our affections and our peace.

EDWIN H. CHAPIN

*Only when grief finds its work done
can God dispense us from it.*

HENRI-FREDERIC AMIEL
Journal

Remember that if the cloud is over you, there is a bright light always on the other side; also that the time is coming, either in this world or the next, when that cloud will be swept away, and the fullness of God's light and wisdom poured around you. God is pledged to keep you as safe as if you could understand everything.   HORACE BUSHNELL

Our joy will sometimes be made sweeter and more wonderful by the very presence of the mourning and the grief. Just as the pillar of cloud, that glided before the Israelites through the wilderness, glowed into a pillar of fire as the darkness deepened, so, as the outlook around becomes less and less cheery and bright, and the night falls thicker and thicker, what seemed to be but a thin, grey, wavering column in the blaze of the sunlight will gather warmth and brightness at the heart of it when the midnight comes.

You cannot see the stars at twelve o'clock in the day; you have to watch for the dark hours ere heaven is filled with glory. And so sorrow is often the occasion for the full revelation of the joy of Christ's presence.   ALEXANDER MACLAREN

*The marvelous richness of human experience
would lose something of rewarding joy
if there were no limitations to overcome.
The hilltop hour would not be half
so wonderful if there were
no dark valleys to traverse.*

Helen Keller
The Story of My Life

For a Time God Seems to Draw Away from Us So We Can Grow Deeper in Our Spiritual Life

The path of the Christian is not always bright with sunshine; he has his seasons of darkness and storm. There are many who have enjoyed the presence of God for a season; they have basked in the sunshine of the earliest stages of their Christian experience; they have walked among the "green pastures" by the side of the "still waters," but suddenly they find their glorious sky is clouded; instead of the land of Goshen they have to tread the sandy desert; in the place of sweet waters, they find troubled streams, bitter to their taste.

The best of God's children must drink from the bitter well; the dearest of His people must bear the cross. No Christian has enjoyed perpetual prosperity; no believer can always keep his harp from the willows. Perhaps the Lord allotted you at first a smooth and unclouded path because you were weak and timid. He tempered the wind for the shorn lamb, but now that you are stronger in the spiritual life, you must enter upon the riper and rougher experience of God's full-grown children.

We need winds and tempests to exercise our faith, to tear off the rotten bough of self-dependence, and to root us more firmly in Christ. The day of evil reveals to us the value of our glorious hope.

Charles H. Spurgeon

Sorrow is better than laughter,
because a sad face is good for the heart.

Ecclesiastes 7:3

Should pain and suffering, sorrow, and grief, rise up like clouds and overshadow for a time the sun of Righteousness and bade Him from your view, do not be dismayed, for in the end this world of woe will descend in showers of blessing on your head, and the sun of Righteousness will rise upon you to set no more for ever (see John 11:20–22).

SUNDAR SINGH
At the Master's Feet

After a time of ever-increasing joy in communion with the Lord, there will come a time of discouragement and uneasiness when we cease to feel the presence of the Lord. We will become distracted and inspirational thoughts will seem to dry up. Our initial fervor and first joyous gifts have been taken away for a time to make room for a deeper calm and peace. The Lord our God is withdrawing from us to allow us to grow deeper in the spiritual life to make us know that without Him we can do nothing, to get us to rely more on Him and His abiding peace. He is preparing our hearts for greater joys which will return after our lessons have been learned.   C. M. M.

There is no stagnancy for the God-directed soul. He is ever guiding us, sometimes with the delicacy of a glance, sometimes with the firmer ministry of a grip, and He moves with us always, even through "the valley of the shadow of death." Therefore, be patient, my soul! The darkness is not your place, the tunnel is not your abiding home! He will bring you out into a large place where you will know "the liberty of the glory of the children of God."

JOHN H. JOWETT

If any one of you be for a time cast down with weariness of spirit or afflicted with aridity of heart so that the torrent of devoted love seem to be dried up. . .realize the Lord's way. For a time He will draw away from you that you may seek Him with great ardor, and having sought may find Him with greater joy, and having found may hold Him with greater love, and having held may never let Him go.

JORDAN OF SAXONY

CLOSING PRAYER

Lord, my God, when the storm is loud,
and the night is dark, and the soul is sad,
and the heart oppressed;
then, weary traveler, may I look to You;
and beholding the light of Your love,
may it bear me on,
until I learn to sing Your song in the night.
Amen.

GEORGE E. DAWSON

CHAPTER 19

Prayer Is Our Desire to Bring Our Will into Harmony with God's Will

The prayer of a righteous man is powerful and effective.

James 5:16

Prayer is an expression of our desire to communicate with God. It aligns us with God's purpose. It leaves us alone with Him to bring us into loving awareness of Him. It is not a matter of changing things externally, but one of working miracles on our inner self. It changes the way we look at things. We pray to make God's will known to us, not to get more, but to be more. Prayer opens the door for God to come in and for self to go out. Why is it so difficult for us to admit that God knows more about what is good for us than we do? He did not remove the "thorn" in Paul's flesh. He did something better. He gave Paul the grace to accept it and to use it to further His kingdom.

What Is Prayer?

This is the high meaning of prayer—not to get things but to realize God. This is the greatest answer to prayer—not bread nor guidance, but comradeship, divine-human comradeship. Real prayer is the journey of the human consciousness, from its absorption in self and things and people, to an awareness of God.   Albert E. Day
Autobiography of Prayer

The object of prayer is to hear the Divine call, and to feel the Divine response to that movement of the soul.

Emily Herman
Creative Prayer

To pray means to revive one's heart, to bid care be gone, to breathe out misery and distress, to breathe in the pure mountain air and the energy of another world.   Paul Wilhelm von Keppler
More Joy

It is not enough to have one contact with God. The true Christian wants to have an abiding fellowship with God. Prayer is the means of realizing this desire. Prayer, then, in its highest sense is an abiding experience of fellowship with God.

C. E. Colton
The Sermon of the Mount

Prayer is as the pitcher that fetcheth water from the brook, therewith to water the herbs: Break the pitcher and it will fetch no water, and for want of water the garden withers.   John Bunyan

Prayer is a rising up and a drawing near to God in mind, and in heart, and in spirit.

Alexander Whyte

Prayer is the simple interchange of thought and feeling with God, rising out of conscious sensuousness into spirituality, turning one's self away from the things of time, and standing upon the threshold of the eternal world.   HENRY WARD BEECHER

Prayer is not hearing yourself talk,
but being silent, staying silent,
and waiting until you hear God.

SOREN KIERKEGAARD

If you remain in me and my words remain in you, ask whatever you wish, and it will be given you."

JOHN 15:7

The soul deep in prayer
As a hyacinth
Stretches forth its pillar of bloom,
Feelers of fragrance unseen,
To the edge of the room.

EVELYN UNDERHILL

The Spirit of Prayer is a pressing forth of the soul out this earthly life. It is a stretching with all its desire after the life of God. WILLIAM LAW
The Spirit of Prayer

Prayer is the soul's sincere desire,
Uttered or unexpressed—
The motion of a hidden fire,
That trembles in the breast.
Prayer is the burden of a sigh,
The falling of a tear,
The upward glancing of an eye,
When none but God is near.

JAMES MONTGOMERY

As soon as we are with God in faith and in love,
we are in prayer.

FRANCOIS FENELON

Prayer is the soul getting into contact with the God in whom it believes.

HARRY EMERSON FOSDICK

*Prayer is a sincere, sensible,
affectionate pouring out of the soul to God,
through Christ in the strength
and assistance of the Spirit,
for such things as God has promised.*

JOHN BUNYAN

Right prayer is not escape from action, it is equipment for action. It is not idle luxury, it is no luxury at all. If anyone ever really has prayed, he knows it is not! It is labor of the most demanding and disciplined variety. It is not a waste of time. The hours spent in communion with God, make better, more effective, the hours spent in action. It is not an effort to get God to do what we ought to do, but to let God equip us for the doing, and help us in the doing and finally to do only what we alone cannot do.

ALBERT E. DAY
An Autobiography of Prayer

The wish to pray is a prayer in itself.

GEORGE BERNANOS
The Diary of a Country Priest

Prayer. . .the very highest energy of which
the mind is capable.

Samuel Taylor Coleridge

Prayer does not consist in an effort to obtain from
God the things which are necessary for this life.
Prayer is an effort to lay hold of God Himself, the
author of life, and when we have found Him who
is the source of life and have entered into communion with Him, then the whole of life is ours.

Sundar Singh
At the Master's Feet

How to Pray

So soon as you wake, retire your mind into a pure
silence from all thoughts and ideas of worldly
things, and in that frame wait upon God to feel
His good presence, to lift up your hearts to Him,
and commit your whole self into His blessed care
and protection.
William Penn
Some Fruits of Solitude

Begin the Day with God
Every morning, lean thine arms awhile
Upon the window-sill of Heaven,
And gaze upon the Lord. . .
Then with that vision in thy heart,
Turn strong to meet the day.

AUTHOR UNKNOWN

Lord! In all my requests I will learn to speak little; to tell Thee my needs simply, that I may thereby humble myself and turn to Thee as the author of all good; and then to hold my peace and await the result of my prayers confidently. Give me simplicity, give me faith, give me love; then whatever may be the method of my prayer it will always be pleasing to Thee and to me always useful. Amen.

JEAN-NICOLAS GROU
How to Pray

Ask and it will be given to you; seek and you will find; knock and the door will be opened to you.

For everyone who asks receives; he who seeks finds; and to him who knocks, the door will be opened."

MATTHEW 7:7–8

This is the fixed, eternal law of the kingdom; if you ask and receive not, it must be because there is something amiss or wanting in the prayer.

ANDREW MURRAY
With Christ in the School of Prayer

Be not forgetful of prayer. Every time you pray, if your prayer is sincere, there will be new feeling and new meaning in it, which will give you fresh courage, and you will understand that prayer is an education.

FYODOR DOSTOEVSKY
The Brothers Karamazov

Do not ask God to do for you that which He has expressly bidden you to do. Ask Him always to help you in every strife, in every service, in every simple act of devotion or obedience you need His help; but do not beseech Him to do your duties for you and to give you without labor those gifts which He has expressly declared shall not be enjoyed except as the fruit of labor.

WASHINGTON GLADDEN
The Christian Way

The Lord's Prayer is
the prayer above all prayers.
It is a prayer which
the most high Master taught us,
wherein are comprehended all
spiritual and temporal blessings,
and the strongest comforts in all trials,
temptations and troubles,
even in the hour of death.

MARTIN LUTHER
Table Talk

You may pray for the release of some areas of life in a friend and find that you are called upon to set right something in your own life that has acted as a stumbling block to him. You may pray that your friend be given courage to endure certain hardships and find that you are drawn to pack your bags and go and join him or that you are to give up your pocket money for the next month or even perhaps to give a fortnight's or a month's salary to help along his cause. In intercessory prayer one seldom ends where one began.

DOUGLAS V. STEERE
Prayer and Worship

The truest prayer begins when we pass beyond word into deep silence, when lips are hushed; when racing thoughts are stilled; when emotions are placid as "the dawning over the waveless ocean."

ALBERT E. DAY
An Autobiography of Prayer

ANSWERS TO OUR PRAYERS OFTEN COME IN UNEXPECTED WAYS

The LORD is near to all who call on him,
to all who call on him in truth.

PSALM 145:18

One obvious reason for our unanswered petitions is, of course, the ignorance of our asking. Piety is no guarantee of wisdom. . . . Indeed, instead of calling prayers unanswered, it is far truer to recognize that "No" is as real an answer as "Yes," and often far more kind. When one considers the partialness of our knowledge, the narrowness of our outlook, our little skill in tracing the far-off consequences of our desire, he sees how often God must speak to us, as Jesus did to the ambitious woman, "Ye know not what ye ask" (Matthew 20:22).

HARRY EMERSON FOSDICK
The Meaning of Prayer

One of the experiences of prayer is that it seems that nothing happens. But when you start with it and look back over a long period of prayer, you suddenly realize that something has happened. What is most close, most intimate, most present, often cannot be experienced directly but only with a certain distance. When I think that I am only distracted, just wasting my time, something is happening too immediate for knowing, understanding, and experiencing. Only in retrospect do I realize that something very important has taken place.

HENRI J. NOUWEN
The Genesee Diary

God's way of answering the Christian's prayer for more patience, experience, hope, and love often is to put him into the furnace of affliction.

RICHARD CECIL

What discord should we bring into the universe if our prayers were all answered. Then we should govern the world and not God. And do you think we should govern it better? It gives me only pain when I hear the long, wearisome petitions of men asking for they know not what. . . . Thanks-giving with a full heart—and the rest silence and submission to the divine will!

Henry Wadsworth Longfellow

Answers to prayer often come in unexpected ways. We pray, for instance, for a certain virtue; but God seldom delivers Christian virtues all wrapped in a package and ready for use. Rather He puts us in situations where by His help we can develop those virtues. Henry Ward Beecher told of a woman who prayed for patience, and God sent her a poor cook. The best answers to prayer may be the vision and strength to meet a circumstance or to assume a responsibility.

C. R. Fidley

To pray is to desire;
but it is to desire what God would have us desire.

Francois Fenelon

Instructions
*G*od answers prayers; sometimes,
    when hearts are weak,
He gives the very gifts believers seek.
But often faith must learn a deeper rest,
And trust God's silence,
    when He does not speak;
For He whose name is Love will send
    the best;
Stars may turn out nor mountain walls endure
But God is true;
His promises are sure to those who seek.

M. G. PLANZ

The one who prays correctly never doubts that the prayer will be answered, even if the very thing for which one prays is not given. For we are to lay our need before God in prayer but not prescribe to God a measure, manner, time, or place. We must leave that to God, for He may wish to give it to us in another, perhaps better, way than we think is best. Frequently we do not know what to pray as St. Paul says in Romans 8, and we know that God's ways are above all that we can ever understand.

MARTIN LUTHER
Table Talk

Prayer is not a lazy substitute for work. It is not a short cut to skill or knowledge. And sometimes God delays the answer to our prayer in final form until we have time to build up the strength, accumulate the knowledge, or fashion the character that would make it possible for Him to say "yes" to what we ask.

ROY M. PEARSON
United Church Herald

He prayed for strength that he might achieve;
He was made weak that he might obey.
He prayed for wealth that he might do
greater things;
He was given poverty that he might be wise.
He prayed for power that he might have the
praise of men;
He was given infirmity that he might feel
the need of God.
He prayed for all things that he might enjoy life;
He was given life that he might enjoy all things.
He had received nothing that he asked for—
all that he hoped for;
His prayer was answered—he was most blessed.

AUTHOR UNKNOWN

Lord, grant us the good
whether we pray for it or not,
but evil keep from us,
even though we pray for it.

Plato

*There is no prayer so blessed as
the prayer which asks nothing.*

Oliver J. Simon
Faith and Experience

What Prayer Does for Us

Even as beginners we all know that the greatest thing that can happen in prayer is a sense of the presence of God. It is the possibility of this experience that makes praying such an exhilarating undertaking. The tiniest moment of feeling lifted into full harmony, of standing on the verge of grasping the meaning of life—even a fleeting experience of such wholeness is so transforming that we take up our daily tasks as if we were new persons.

Marguerite Harmon Bro
More Than We Are

Prayer unites the soul to God.

JULIANA OF NORWICH

Prayer is so necessary and
the source of so much good,
that the soul which has found this treasure
cannot resist returning to it when left to itself.

FRANCOIS FENELON
Instructions

Though God knows all our needs, prayer is necessary for the cleansing and enlightenment of our soul. It is well to stand in the sunshine: It is warm and light; likewise, when standing in prayer before God, our spiritual sun, we are warmed and enlightened. JOHN SERGIEFF
(JOHN OF CRONSTADT)
My Life in Christ

The function of prayer is
to set God at the center of attention.

ALBERT E. DAY
An Autobiography of Prayer

Deep in every one of us lies the tendency to pray. If we allow it to remain merely a tendency, it becomes nothing but a selfish, unintelligent, occasional cry of need. But understood and disciplined, it reveals possibilities whose limits never have been found.

HARRY EMERSON FOSDICK
The Meaning of Prayer

*Call to me and I will answer you
and tell you great and unsearchable things
you do not know."*

JEREMIAH 33:3

Fill yourselves first and then
only will you be able to give to others.

AUGUSTINE OF HIPPO

*Prayer does not change God,
but changes him who prays.*

SOREN KIERKEGAARD
Works of Love

The Christian who prays, recollects himself,
that is to say he discovers himself,
gathers himself together,
frees himself from all useless masters,
from all unknown hands,
from all fast-holding desires which
tear him to pieces and so prevent him
from being himself.

PIERRE CHARLES
Prayer for All Times

Probably the greatest result of the life of prayer is an unconscious but steady growth into the knowledge of the mind of God and into conformity with His will; for after all, prayer is not so much the means whereby God's will is bent to man's desires, as it is that whereby man's will is bent to God's desires.

CHARLES H. BRENT

CLOSING PRAYER

Lord, I do not know what to ask of You;
only You know what I need;
You love me better than I know how to love myself.
I simply present myself before You;
I open my heart to You.
Behold my needs which I know not myself;
see, and do according to Your tender mercy.
I adore all your purposes without knowing them;
I yield myself to You;
I should have no other desire
than to accomplish Your will.
Teach me to pray.
Amen.

FRANCOIS FENELON

CHAPTER 20

THE BIBLE IS GOD
REVEALING HIMSELF TO US

*"The words I have spoken to you
are spirit and they are life."*

JOHN 6:63

Jesus Christ is the key to understanding the whole of the Scriptures. They point to Jesus and illuminate the nature of God's revelation of Himself through Jesus. From the very beginning, starting with Abraham, it is the story of God's redemption of mankind through Jesus Christ, the story of leading mankind to Him, to a loving relationship with Him. The hundreds of people of the Bible are clamoring out for us to hear the message of salvation destined for us. One voice speaks out as no other voice. It speaks to the deepest need of our hearts. Jesus whispers our name and says, "Come unto me all of you and I will give you rest." The Bible contains all the wisdom necessary for mankind. If we read God's Word again and again with faith and love until it comes alive in us, penetrating the deepest levels of our mind, then the right words will come to us whenever we need a word of encouragement from God. This is one way He speaks to us.

GOD HAS SPOKEN TO US SO THAT OUR JOY MAY BE IN HIM AND IT MAY BE FULL

The central theme of the Bible is Jesus Christ. It begins with Jesus Christ as the bud in Genesis that produces the flower, the finished fruit in Revelation, the coming, ruling King of kings. The Old Testament conceals Christ, the New Testament reveals Christ. The Old Testament veils Christ, the New Testament unveils Christ. The Old Testament is Christ concealed, the New Testament is Christ revealed. The Old Testament contains Christ, the New Testament explains Christ. It is, indeed, "The Jesus Book."   JOHN R. BISAGNO

Every light that comes from Holy Scripture comes from the light of grace. This is why foolish, proud and learned people are blind even in the light, because the light is clouded by their own pride and selfish love. They read the Scripture literally, not with understanding. They have let go of the light by which the Scripture was formed and proclaimed.

CATHERINE OF SIENA

The Bible is a vivid,
sometimes parabolic account of
God's persistent,
unrelenting quest for us
and our stumbling,
often faithless response.

GEORGE CORNELL
The Untamed God

The Bible is a window in this prison of hope, through which we look into eternity.

JOHN S. DWIGHT

The sacred writings are the principal source of all that God is pleased to reveal to us of His essence and perfections, His natural and supernatural works, His designs regarding man, the end He wills him to attain, and the means conducive to that end. Therein we see that God is the beginning of all things; that He governs all and intends all for His glory, and has accomplished all things for Himself, there being no other end possible for Him.

JEAN-NICOLAS GROU
Spiritual Maxims

All men are like grass,
and all their glory is like
the flowers of the field;
the grass withers and the flowers fall,
but the word of the Lord stands forever."

1 PETER 1:24–25

The word of God will stand a thousand readings;
and he who has gone over it most frequently is
the surest of finding new wonders there.

J. HAMILTON

Just as all things upon earth
represent and image forth
all the realities of another world,
so the Bible is one mighty representative of the
whole spiritual life of humanity.

HELEN KELLER

*The Bible becomes ever more beautiful
the more it is understood.*

JOHANN WOLFGANG VON GOETHE
Wilhelm Meister's Travels

The book wherein, for thousands of years,
the spirit of man has found
light and nourishment,
and the response to
whatever was deepest in his heart.

THOMAS CARLYLE

In the beginning God created heaven and earth and all they contain. The crown jewel of His creative work was mankind, created in His own image for fellowship with Himself. Mankind chose to disobey God, however. As humanity chose a path of sin, a great rift opened separating sinful mankind from Holy God. The Bible is the story of God's plan to bridge that rift and bring mankind back to Himself. It began with a man named Abraham whom God promised to make a blessing to the entire world. It was through his descendants that salvation would come. Every other person and event in the Old Testament pointed to the future gift of a renewed relationship with God. The religious rites and sacrifices of Old Testament religion were mere precursors to the gift of salvation to come. The prophets indicated the gift would come in the form of a person called "Messiah," or "Anointed One." Every law and commandment in the Old Testament prepared the way for His coming.

The Gospels, the climax of the biblical story, tell of the birth and life of Jesus the Messiah. He proclaimed that in Himself all of the law and prophets were fulfilled. He came to show us the way to God through His sinless life and profound teaching. At the very peak of His ministry He allowed Himself to be falsely arrested and crucified. What seemed certain defeat to the world was the ultimate step in God's plan. Jesus, in His sinlessness, became the ultimate sacrifice for sin and paved the way for humanity to have a renewed relationship with God. The remainder of the New Testament records instruction and encouragement to spread the news of Jesus to the entire world. The great proclamation of the New Testament is that whoever believes in Him will not perish but have eternal life. The Bible ends with a look to the future. The promise of Christ's future return points to the eventual conclusion of God's plan, that all who would trust in Him will spend eternity with Him in Heaven, and all who would not will be eternally judged in Hades. Thus God's plan, certain before creation began, will be perfectly complete.

RON G. MARSH
Sermons

The Bible is God's chart for you to steer by,
to keep you from the bottom of the sea,
and to show you where the harbor is,
and how to reach it without
running on rocks and bars.

HENRY WARD BEECHER

The Bible is a book for the mind, the heart, the conscience, the will, and the life. It suits the palace and the cottage, the afflicted and the prosperous, the living and the dying. It is a comfort to "the house of mourning," and a check to "the house of feasting." It "giveth seed to the sower, and bread to the eater." It is simple, yet grand; mysterious, yet plain; and though from God, it is, nevertheless, within the comprehension of a little child.

T. L. HAINES
The Royal Path of Life

We search the world for truth. We cull
The good, the true, the beautiful,
From graven stone and written scroll,
And all old flower-fields of the soul
And, weary seekers of the best,
We come back laden from our quest,
To find that all the sages said
Is in the Book our mothers read.

JOHN GREENLEAF WHITTIER

The word of God is living and active.
Sharper than any double-edged sword,
it penetrates even to dividing soul and spirit,
joints and marrow;
it judges the thoughts and attitudes
of the heart.

HEBREWS 4:12

As the rain and the snow come down from heaven, and do not return to it without watering the earth and making it bud and flourish, so that it yields seed for the sower and bread for the eater, so is my word that goes out from my mouth: It will not return to me empty, but will accomplish what I desire and achieve the purpose for which I sent it."

ISAIAH 55:10–11

CLOSING PRAYER

Father, let Your word be a lamp to my feet,
and a light to my path.
Let me hide it in my heart that
I might not sin against You.
Amen.

CHAPTER 21

THE GIFT OF GOD IS ETERNAL LIFE

"I tell you the truth,
whoever hears my word
and believes him who sent me
has eternal life and will not be condemned;
he has crossed over from death to life."

JOHN 5:24

All mankind is of one Author, and is one volume; when one man dies, one chapter is not torn out of the book, but translated into a better language; and every chapter must be so translated; God employs several translators; some pieces are translated by age, some by sickness, some by war, some by justice; but God's hand is in every translation; and His hand shall bind up all our scattered leaves again, for that library where every book shall lie open to one another. JOHN DONNE

GOD HAS SET ETERNITY
IN OUR HEARTS

*Our Lord has written the promise
of the resurrection,
not in books alone,
but in every leaf in springtime.*

MARTIN LUTHER

What reason have atheists for saying that we cannot rise again? Which is the more difficult, to be born, or to rise again? That what has never been, should be, or that what has been, should be again? Is it more difficult to come into being than to return to it? BLAISE PASCAL

Pensees

I feel within me the future life. I am like a forest that has once been razed; the new shoots are stronger and brisker. I shall most certainly rise toward the heavens. The sun's rays bathe my head. The earth gives me its generous sap, but the heavens illuminate me with the reflection of—of worlds unknown.

Some say the soul results merely from bodily powers. Why, then, does my soul become brighter when my bodily powers begin to waste away? Winter is above me, but eternal spring is within my heart. I inhale even now the fragrance of lilies, violets, and roses just as I did when I was twenty. The nearer my approach to the end, the plainer is the sound of immortal symphonies of worlds which invite me. It is wonderful, yet simple. It is a fairy tale; it is history.   VICTOR HUGO

It is scarcely possible that
a misleading instinct would be implanted
in all men in all ages.

OWEN P. EACHES

Our Creator would never have made such lovely days and have given us the deep hearts to enjoy them, above and beyond all thought, unless we were meant to be immortal.   NATHANIEL HAWTHORNE

But when once we have perceived the truth, that the body is not ourselves, but the habitation of the soul, we can make it into an instrument of our development.

ARTHUR CHRISTOPHER BENSON
The Silent Isle

The hunger and thirst of immortality is upon the human soul, filling it with aspirations and desires for higher better things than the world can give. We can never be fully satisfied but in God.

TRYON EDWARDS

It has now been revealed through the appearing of our Savior, Christ Jesus, who has destroyed death and has brought life and immortality to light through the gospel.   2 TIMOTHY 1:10

Whence this pleasing hope, this fond desire,
This longing for immortality?
'Tis the divinity that stirs within us.
'Tis heaven itself that points out an hereafter,
And intimates eternity to man.

Joseph Addison

Before long,
the world will not see me anymore,
but you will see me.
Because I live, you also will live."

John 14:19

Why should any of you consider it incredible
that God raises the dead?"

Acts 26:8

We are no more responsible for the idea of
immortality in the heart than for the eye
of physical vision in the head.

Karl Reiland

Would any God who breathes in us such need
And power to learn of Him, who let us look
Upon some pages freely, bid us read
The preface only—and then shut the book?

ADELAIDE LOVE
from "For a Materialist"

God has written this truth of immortality in our own personal lives and experiences. We have certain instincts, certain longings and desires, certain unrest, unfulfilled yearnings; these will find their answer, their corresponding element elsewhere. These undeveloped powers of our being will come to fruition, to completion yonder. The incomplete life demands a future life.   E. C. SCHAEFFER

WE HAVE AN ETERNAL HOUSE IN HEAVEN
NOT BUILT WITH HUMAN HANDS

The truest end of life is to know
the life that never ends.

WILLIAM PENN
Some Fruits of Solitude

We are like deep sea divers moving slowly and clumsily in the dim twilight of the depths, and we have our work to do. But this is not our element, and the relief of the diver in coming back to fresh air and sunlight and the sight of familiar faces is but a poor picture of the unspeakable delight with which we shall emerge from our necessary imprisonment into the loveliness and satisfaction of our true home.

J. B. PHILLIPS
Making Men Whole

You are a little soul bearing about a corpse.

EPICTETUS

If a man that is desperately sick today,
did believe he should arise sound
the next morning;
or a man today, in despicable poverty,
had assurance that he should
tomorrow arise a prince;
would they be afraid to go to bed?

RICHARD BAXTER

Our home is—Heaven.
On earth we are like travelers staying at a hotel.
When one is away,
one is always thinking of going home.

JOHN VIANNEY

Divine wisdom, intending to detain us some time on earth, has done well to cover with a veil the prospect of the life to come; for if our sight could clearly distinguish the opposite bank, who would remain on this tempestuous coast of time?

ANNE GERMAINE DE STAEL

I am the resurrection and the life.
He who believes in me. . .will never die."

JOHN 11:25–26

Christianity is a religion of the open tomb.

ROY L. SMITH
The Methodist Story

Death is not a journeying
in to an unknown land;
it is a voyage home.
We are going
not to a strange country,
but to our Father's house,
and among our kith and kin.

JOHN RUSKIN

The resurrection of Jesus Christ is our hope today. It is our assurance that we have a living Savior to help us live as we should now, and that when, in the end, we set forth on that last great journey, we shall not travel an uncharted course, but rather we shall go on a planned voyage—life to death to eternal living.

RAYMOND MACKENDREE
Queens' Gardens

Now we know that if
the earthly tent we live in is destroyed,
we have a building from God,
an eternal house in heaven,
not built by human hands.

2 CORINTHIANS 5:1

Those are dead even for this life
who hope for no other.

JOHANN WOLFGANG VON GOETHE

So live that when thy summons comes to join
The innumerable caravan which moves
To that mysterious realm where each shall take
His chamber in the silent halls of death,
Thou goest not, like the quarry-slave at night,
Scourged to his dungeon, but sustained
and soothed
By an unfaltering trust, approach thy grave
Like one that wraps the drapery of his couch
About him, and lies down to pleasant dreams.

WILLIAM CULLEN BRYANT
"Thanatopsis"

This life is only a prelude to eternity.
For that which we call death is but a pause,
in truth a progress into life.

LUCIUS ANNAEUS SENECA

Spring itself is Resurrection!
Bough and bud combine to prove
That death is a temporal imperfection
Through which all of life must move.

RALPH W. SEAGER

Now we see but a poor reflection as in a mirror;
then we shall see face to face.
Now I know in part; then I shall know fully,
even as I am fully known.

1 CORINTHIANS 13:12

Day is done, gone the sun
From the lake, from the hills, from the sky.
Safely rest, all is well! God is nigh.

AUTHOR UNKNOWN

Death? Translated into the heavenly tongue,
that word means life!

HENRY WARD BEECHER
Life Thoughts

They that love beyond the world cannot be separated by it. Death cannot kill what never dies, nor can spirits ever be divided that love and live in the same divine principle.

WILLIAM PENN
Some Fruits of Solitude

This life is but the passage of a day,
This life is but a pang and all is over;
But in the life to come which fades not away
Every love shall abide and every lover.

CHRISTINA GEORGINA ROSSETTI
Saints and Angels

Joy, shipmate, joy!
(Pleased to my soul at death I cry),
Our life is closed, our life begins,
The long, long anchorage we leave,
The ship is clear at last, she leaps!
She swiftly courses from the shore,
Joy, shipmate, joy!

WALT WHITMAN

Death is not extinguishing the light;
it is only putting out the lamp
because the Dawn has come.

RABINDRANATH TAGORE

And this is the testimony: God has given us eternal life, and this life is in his Son. He who has the Son has life; he who does not have the Son of God does not have life. I write these things to you who believe in the name of the Son of God so that you may know that you have eternal life.

1 JOHN 5:11–13

CLOSING PRAYER

Lord, grant that I may seek rather
To comfort than to be comforted
To understand than to be understood
To love than to be loved;
For it is by giving that one receives,
It is by self-forgetting that one finds,
It is by forgiving that one is forgiven,
It is by dying that one awakens to eternal life.

FRANCIS OF ASSISI

PART SIX

THE GIVING SOUL—
THE OUTWARD JOURNEY,
EXPANDING IN GROWTH
TO INCLUDE OTHERS

One of the principal rules of religion is,
to lose no occasion of serving God.
And since He is invisible to our eyes,
we are to serve Him in our neighbor
which He receives as if done to Himself in person,
standing visibly before us.

JOHN WESLEY

CHAPTER 22

KINDNESS SHOWN TO OTHERS DEMONSTRATES OUR LOVE FOR GOD AND DOES GOOD TO OUR OWN SOUL

Get rid of all bitterness, rage and anger,
brawling and slander,
along with every form of malice.
Be kind and compassionate to one another.

EPHESIANS 4:31–32

All the teachings of the Bible about our relationship to our fellow man could be summed up in the Golden Rule. Let us learn from Jesus. His whole life was a giving of self to others, an unspeakable kindness of heart. Let us be kind and compassionate to each other, always living for the other, not ourselves, as Jesus did. Kind words can heal the wounded heart and uplift the downtrodden spirit. Expect the best of people and often they will live up to your expectations. An atmosphere of love thus created will propagate more love and generosity. If we would just realize that in our dealings with others we are dealing with the Lord Himself, how quickly we would show mercy to all human frailty and weakness. Wanting the best for others is in essence wanting the best for oneself. The hearts which show mercy, which have pity for all frailty and the generosity to help, will know that they are participating in a divine encounter.

WHAT GOOD IS IT IF WE CAN SEE AND HEAR
IF OUR HEARTS ARE BLIND AND DEAF?

*If I can put one thought of rosy sunset into
the life of any man or woman,
I shall feel that I have worked with God.*

GEORGE MACDONALD

The alien living with you must be treated
as one of your native-born. Love him as yourself."

LEVITICUS 19:34

I expect to pass through this world but once. Any good work, therefore, any kindness, or any service I can render to any soul of man or animal, let me do it now! Let me not neglect or defer it, for I shall not pass this way again.

Edward, Earl of Devon

Opportunities of doing kindness are often lost from mere want of thought. Half a dozen lines of kindness may bring sunshine into the whole day of some sick person. Think of the pleasure you might give to some one who is much shut up, and who has fewer pleasures than you have, by sharing with her some little comfort or enjoyment that you have learnt to look upon as a necessity of life,—the pleasant drive, the new book, flowers from the country, etc. Try to put yourself in another's place. Ask "What should I like myself, if I were hard-worked, or sick, or lonely?" Cultivate the habit of sympathy.

George H. Wilkinson

A cup of cold water"—a little thing! But life is made up of little things, and he who would rise to higher usefulness is wise if he cherishes the loving yet seeming trifles of daily living.

Floyd W. Tomkins

I see from my house by the side of
    the road,
By the side of the highway of life,
The men who press with the ardor of hope,
The men who faint with strife;
But I turn not away from their smiles nor
    their tears—
Both parts of an infinite plan—
Let me live in a house by the side of
    the road
And be a friend to man.

SAM WALTER FOSS,
from "The House by the Side of the Road"

The best part of a good man's life,
His little, nameless unremembered acts
Of kindness and of love.

WILLIAM WORDSWORTH

*T*rust men and they will be true to you;
    treat them greatly and
    they will show themselves great.

RALPH WALDO EMERSON

Kind words are the music of the world. They have a power which seems to be beyond natural causes, as if they are some angel's song which had lost its way and come on earth. It seems as if they could almost do what in reality God alone can do—soften the hard and angry hearts of men. No one was ever corrected by a sarcasm—crushed, perhaps, if the sarcasm was clever enough—but drawn nearer to God, never.   FREDERICK W. FABER

Let us learn the lessons Christ so beautifully taught, and so faithfully exemplified. He fed all the multitude and healed all the sick that were in all their coast; and from the cross He threw out the hands of sympathy and supplication, even for the infuriated mob who were delighting in His agonies and mocking at His death. . . . This is for our imitation for He says, if thine enemy hunger, feed him; and if he thirst, give him drink; and pray for those who despitefully use you and persecute you.   J. B. MOODY

Be kind,
for every one you meet is fighting a battle.

JOHN WATSON

As we meet and touch, each day,
The many travelers on our way,
Let every such brief contact be
A glorious, helpful ministry;
The contact of the soil and seed,
Each giving to the other's best,
And blessing, each, as well as blest.

SUSAN COOLIDGE

The spirit of good-will, of affection, of loving understanding, generously expressed can never fail to make a place for us in the hearts of others. Often the most austere and forbidding are most hungry for the word of friendliness or encouragement that is in our power to bestow. One has only to try the experiment for a day to prove its truth. Even the slightest gesture of kindliness to each person we come in contact with for twenty-four hours will bring astonishing results. A quick smile, a kindling eye, a gracious response are almost certain to follow.

A spirit of never-failing love, of interior peace, and joy that wells from the divinely fed springs of one's being cannot fail to find infinite opportunities for service, and the wisdom and power to meet them.

ALICE HEGAN RICE
My Pillow Book

Correction does much,
but encouragement does more.
Encouragement after censure is
as the sun after a shower.

JOHANN WOLFGANG VON GOETHE

IN EVERYTHING,
DO TO OTHERS WHAT YOU WOULD HAVE
THEM DO TO YOU

No man can be a friend of Jesus Christ
who is not a friend to his neighbor.

R. H. BENSON
The Friendship of Christ

I tell you the truth, whatever you did for one of the
least of these brothers of mine, you did for me."

MATTHEW 25:40

Sincerity includes the self-restraint which refuses to make capital of others' faults; the charity which delights not in exposing the weakness of others, but "covereth all things."   HENRY DRUMMOND
The Greatest Thing in the World

Charity does not demand of us that we should not see the faults of others; we must in that case shut our eyes. But it commands us to avoid attending unnecessarily to them, and that we be not blind to the good, while we are so clear-sighted to the evil that exists. We must remember, too, God's continual kindness to the most worthless creature, and think how many causes we have to think ill of ourselves; and finally we must consider that charity embraces the very lowest human being. It acknowledges that in the sight of God the contempt that we indulge for others has in its very nature a harshness and arrogance opposed to the spirit of Jesus Christ.

FRANCOIS FENELON

He who is kind to the poor lends to the LORD.
PROVERBS 19:17

The rule for doing unto others as you would wish them to do unto you calls for no miraculous proof, neither does it require faith because the rule is convincing in itself, both to reason and to human nature.

Leo Tolstoy
The Complete Works of Leo Tolstoy

*When you defend those who are absent,
you retain the trust of those present.*

Stephen Covey
The Seven Habits of Highly Effective People

With our neighbor there is life and death:
for if we do good to our brother,
we shall do good to God;
but if we scandalize our brother,
we sin against Christ.

Anthony

A KIND MAN BENEFITS HIMSELF,
BUT A CRUEL MAN BRINGS HIMSELF HARM

It is a very small matter to you whether the man give you your right or not; it is life or death to you whether or not you give him his. Whether he pay you what you count his debt or not, you will be compelled to pay him all you owe him. If you owe him a pound and he you a million, you must pay him the pound whether he pay you the million or not; there is no business-parallel here. If, owing you love, he gives you hate, you, owing him love, have yet to pay it.   GEORGE MACDONALD

A man who habitually pleases himself will be continually more selfish and sordid, even among the most noble and beautiful conditions which nature, history, or art can furnish; and, on the other hand, any one who will try each day to live for the sake of others, will grow more and more gracious in thought and bearing, however dull and even squalid may be the outward circumstances of his soul's probation.   FRANCIS PAGET

Doing nothing for others is the undoing of one's self. We must be purposely kind and generous, or we miss the best part of existence. The heart that goes out of itself, gets large and full of joy. This is the great secret of the inner life. We do ourselves the most good doing something for others.

HORACE MANN

It is one of the most beautiful compensations
of this life that no man can sincerely help
another without helping himself.

RALPH WALDO EMERSON

He that does good to another
does good also to himself,
not only in the consequence
but in the very act.
For the consciousness of well-doing is
in itself ample reward.

LUCIUS ANNAEUS SENECA

KIND DEEDS THAT ARE HIDDEN
ARE MOST MEANINGFUL

If someone else is well spoken of,
be more pleased than if it were yourself;
this is easy enough for
if you were really humble,
it would vex you to be praised.

TERESA OF AVILA
The Interior Castle

The human eye I seek is like the scorching ray that destroys all the delicate colors in the most costly material. Every action that is done, only to be seen of others, loses its freshness in the sight of God, like the flower that passing through many hands is at last hardly presentable.

Oh, my soul! be as the desert flower that grows, blooms, and flourishes unseen, in obedience to God's Will, and cares not whether the passing bird perceives it, or the wind scatters the petals, scarcely formed.   *Gold Dust*

We weaken the value of our gifts of service by adding to it love of praise of others, honor, or material profit. Our goal is simply the love of God, without any other consideration whatsoever. Not only does this unseen service help the individual being served and especially the one serving, but it also helps people who know nothing of them. Seeing this act of unselfish giving, they are encouraged to do little acts of kindness themselves. They sense that the real motive behind the service runs far deeper than the service act and are thus inspired in their own faith.   C. M. M.

He who careth for
neither praises nor reproaches
hath great tranquillity of heart.

THOMAS À KEMPIS
The Imitation of Christ

CLOSING PRAYER

O Lord, You are the Way,
the Truth, and the Life,
we lift our hearts to You.
Guide us in the Way this day,
enlighten us with the Truth,
and grant us the more abundant Life
which You alone can give.
This we ask, not that we may selfishly
get good or glory for ourselves,
but that we may do good unto
others and so glorify Your name.
Amen.

HOWARD B. GROSE

CHAPTER 23

JUDGING OTHERS MEANS WE OURSELVES ARE IN NEED OF CORRECTION

*"If any one of you is without sin,
let him be the first to throw a stone."*

JOHN 8:7

We are always wanting to change others, but often forget to look at our own need for inner change. Jesus had a lot to say about the self-righteous hypocrite who condemned others without seeing the "board" in his own eye. We should examine ourselves for a long time before we even consider judging another. The way we act toward others will be determined by our faithfulness to Jesus Christ and our relationship to Him. A hurtful act towards another represents the utter poverty we feel in ourselves. When we discover an offensive personality trait in someone else which causes us to over-react, the chances are we have become blinded to it in ourselves. The more arrogance or deceitfulness or cruelty we exhibit, the more we dislike it in others. We all try to hide our weaknesses because in admitting them we fear exposing ourselves to ridicule. So we point to others' mistakes, inconsistencies and wrongdoings. This, we hope, will make our own inadequacies look better. Of course, this does not work. Instead of finding fault, let us look to find the good in others.

WE WOULD NOT NOTICE DEFECTS
IN OTHERS IF WE WERE NOT
UNCONSCIOUSLY GUILTY IN SOME WAY
OF THE SAME FAULTS

Our judgment of others is usually faulty and inaccurate because our own vision is marred by obstacles as great, if not greater, than those which we think we see in the lives of others. By pointing out the faults of others the critic hopes to turn the attention of others away from his own sins.   C. E. COLTON
The Sermon on the Mount

You, therefore, have no excuse, you who pass judgment on someone else, for at whatever point you judge the other, you are condemning yourself, because you who pass judgment do the same things.

ROMANS 2:1

Everything that is unconscious in ourselves we discover in our neighbor and we treat him accordingly. We no longer subject him to the test of drinking poison; we do not burn him or put screws on him; but we injure him by means of moral verdicts pronounced with the deepest conviction. What we combat in him is usually our own inferior side.

CARL G. JUNG

Search thy own heart; what paineth thee in others in thyself may be found.

JOHN GREENLEAF WHITTIER

If we had no faults, we should not take so much pleasure in noticing them in others.

FRANCOIS DE LA ROCHEFOUCAULD

Study to be patient in bearing the defects of others, because you also have many things which others must bear. We want others strictly corrected, and are not willing to be corrected ourselves. But God has so ordered it, that we may learn to bear one another's burdens, for there is no man without defect, no man sufficient for himself. We must support, comfort, help, instruct, and admonish one another. The amount of each man's virtue better appears on occasion of adversity: For the occasions do not make a man frail—they reveal what he is!

THOMAS À KEMPIS
The Imitation of Christ

LET US JUDGE OURSELVES BEFORE
WE EVEN CONSIDER JUDGING OTHERS AND
THEN WE WILL NOT WANT TO JUDGE THEM

When the actions of a neighbor are upon the stage, we can have all our wits about us, are so quick and critical we can split a hair and find out every failure and infirmity, but are without feeling or have but very little sense of our own. WILLIAM PENN
Some Fruits of Solitude

*Everybody thinks of changing humanity
and nobody thinks of changing himself.*

LEO TOLSTOY

There is no true and constant gentleness without humility; while we are so fond of ourselves, we are easily offended with others. Let us be persuaded that nothing is due to us, and then nothing will disturb us. Let us often think of our own infirmities, and we shall become indulgent towards those of others.   FRANCOIS FENELON

*When I feel like finding fault
I always begin with myself
and then I never get any farther.*

DAVID GRAYSON
Adventures in Friendship

Oftentimes too we do not perceive our own inward blindness, how great it is. We often do evil, and excuse it worse. We are sometimes moved with passion, and we think it to be zeal. We reprehend small things in others, and pass over greater matters in ourselves. We quickly enough feel and weigh what we suffer at the hands of others; but we mind not what others suffer from us. He that well and rightly considereth his own works will find little cause to judge harshly of another.   THOMAS À KEMPIS
The Imitation of Christ

No one in this world is so perfect that if he were to examine his own heart, he would not find sin enough of which to rid himself, so that he would not be able justly to reprove others. In judging others a man labors in vain; he often errs, and easily falls into sin; but in judging and examining himself he always labors to good purpose.   JOHANNES TAULER
The Inner Way

Look that you yourself are in order, and leave to God the task of unraveling the skein of the world and of destiny.   HENRI-FREDERIC AMIEL
Journal

How good it would be if we could learn to be rigorous in judgment of ourselves, and gentle in our judgment of our neighbors! In remedying defects, kindness works best with others, sternness with ourselves. It is easy to make allowances for our faults, but dangerous; hard to make allowances for others' faults, but wise. "If thy hand offend thee, cut it off," are words for our sins; for the sins of others, "Father, forgive them."

MALTBIE D. BABCOCK
Thoughts for Every-Day Living

Why do you look at the speck of sawdust in your brother's eye and pay no attention to the plank in your own eye? How can you say to your brother, 'Let me take the speck out of your eye,' when all the time there is a plank in your own eye? You hypocrite, first take the plank out of your own eye, and then you will see clearly to remove the speck from your brother's eye."

MATTHEW 7:3–5

We find fault with our neighbor very readily for a small matter, while we pass over great things in ourselves. We strive to sell dear and buy cheap. We are eager to deal out strict justice to others, but to obtain indulgence for ourselves. We expect a good construction to be put on all we say, but we are sensitive and critical to our neighbor's words. We have enough to do in judging ourselves without undertaking to judge our neighbors.

FRANCIS DE SALES
Introduction to the Devout Life

CLOSING PRAYER

*Forgive us if this day we have done or said any-
thing to increase the pain of the world.
Pardon the judgmental attitude, the unkind word,
the impatient gesture, the hard and selfish deed, the
failure to show sympathy
and kindly help where we had the opportunity,
but missed it.
Amen.*

FREDERICK B. MEYER

CHAPTER 24

Let Us Love One Another
Because Love Comes from God

*If we love one another, God lives
in us and his love is made complete in us.*

1 John 4:12

For twenty centuries, millions of people have drawn from God's flame of love a passionate fervor and have renounced every other ambition and every other joy except that of abandoning themselves to God's love. Our love of neighbor is the measure of our love of God. It means an openness and receptivity to our fellow man, a readiness to help without reserve. It means living not for ourselves, but for others. The power of love was the moral of all of Jesus' parables. It is the one thing we have to learn.

It is all. Negativity on the part of humankind is a cry for love. If we really understood this, how quickly we would respond with love instead of criticism. To love where one is not loved—that is the miracle and can only be accomplished through the power of Jesus' blood. The true test of all our words and actions is—are they inspired by love? "All men shall know that you are my disciples because you have love towards one another."

WE NEED TO BE ROOTED
AND ESTABLISHED IN LOVE

We receive the Holy Spirit, and the fruit of the spirit is love, joy, peace, longsuffering, gentleness, goodness, faith, meekness, self-control, and "against such things there is no law" (Galatians 5:22–23). Therefore, one who has the new heart doesn't need any law because the Holy Spirit makes the law unnecessary. This is why Jesus said that all the law and the prophets are fulfilled in one word, love.   JUAN CARLOS ORTIZ
Living with Jesus Today

All true morality, inward and outward, is comprehended in love, for love is the foundation of all the commandments. . . . There is no inner freedom which does not manifest itself in works of love.

MEISTER ECKHART
Sermons

Love unites the soul with God:
and the more love the soul has
the more powerfully it enters into God
and is centered on Him.

JOHN OF THE CROSS
The Living Flame of Love

There is no surprise more magical than
the surprise of being loved;
it is God's finger on a man's shoulder.

CHARLES MORGAN

Love is ever the beginning of knowledge
as fire is of light.

THOMAS CARLYLE

Love is patient, love is kind. It does not envy, it does not boast, it is not proud. It is not rude, it is not self-seeking, it is not easily angered, it keeps no record of wrongs. Love does not delight in evil but rejoices with the truth. It always protects, always trusts, always hopes, always perseveres. Love never fails.   1 CORINTHIANS 13:4–8

The whole gist of the matter lies in the will, and this is what our Dear Lord meant by saying, "The Kingdom of God is within you." It is not a question of how much we know, how clever we are, nor even how good; it all depends upon the heart's love. External actions are the results of love, the fruit it bears; but the source, the root, is in the deep of the heart.   FRANCOIS FENELON

Jesus replied: " 'Love the Lord your God with all your heart and with all your soul and with all your mind.' This is the first and greatest commandment. And the second is like it: 'Love your neighbor as yourself.' All the Law and the Prophets hang on these two commandments."

MATTHEW 22:37–40

*The love we give away
is the only love we keep.*

JOHN WOODS

It is love that asks, that seeks,
that knocks, that finds,
and that is faithful to what it finds.

AUGUSTINE OF HIPPO

WE HAVE PASSED FROM DEATH TO LIFE
BECAUSE WE LOVE OUR BROTHERS

After you have been kind, after love has stolen
forth into the world and done its beautiful work,
go back into the shade again and say nothing
about it. Love hides even from itself. Love waives
even self-satisfaction. "Love vaunteth not itself, is
not puffed up."

HENRY DRUMMOND
The Greatest Thing in the World

There are two loves from which all good and truth come: love of the Lord and love of the neighbor. And there are two loves from which all evils and falsities come: the love of self and the love of the world.   EMANUEL SWEDENBORG

By loving our neighbor we show our love of God. Isn't that the exact measure of our love of God? Who, then, is our neighbor? It is anyone who shows up in our life who needs our help. The Good Samaritan happened to come across a man by the side of the road who had fallen among thieves and needed his help. God's love of all people is the reason for loving the one in need that He sends to us personally to minister unto. That makes it a personal act, love given person to person, not just love of people as a whole.   C. M. M.

The surest way to determine whether one possesses the love of God is to see whether he loves his neighbor. These two loves are never separated. Rest assured, the more you progress in love of neighbor the more your love of God will increase.

                    TERESA OF AVILA

Let us see that whenever we have failed to be loving, we have also failed to be wise; that whenever we have been blind to our neighbor's interest, we have also been blind to our own; whenever we have hurt others, we have hurt ourselves still more. Let us, at this blessed Whitsuntide, ask forgiveness of God for all acts of malice and uncharitableness, blindness and hardness of heart; and pray for the spirit of true charity, which alone is true wisdom. And let us come to Holy Communion in charity with each other and with all; determined henceforth to feel for each other, and with each other; to put ourselves in our neighbors' places; to see with their eyes, and to feel with their hearts, so far as God shall give us that great grace; determined to make allowances for their mistakes and failings; to give and forgive, even as God gives and forgives, for ever; that so we may be indeed the children of our Father in heaven, whose name is Love.   CHARLES KINGSLEY

We love because he first loved us. If anyone says, "I love God," yet hates his brother, he is a liar. For anyone who does not love his brother, whom he has seen, cannot love God, whom he has not seen. And he has given us this command: Whoever loves God must also love his brother.   1 JOHN 4:19–21

If religion commands universal charity, to love our neighbor as ourselves, to forgive and pray for all our enemies without any reserve; it is because all degrees of love are degrees of happiness, that strengthen and support the Divine life of the soul, and are as necessary to its health and happiness, as proper food is necessary to the health and happiness of the body.   WILLIAM LAW
A Serious Call to a Devout and Holy Life

You have enemies; for who can live on this earth without them? Take heed to yourselves: Love them. In no way can your enemy so hurt you by his violence as you hurt yourself if you love him not. And let it not seem to you impossible to love him. Believe first that it can be done, and pray the will of God may be done in you. For what good can your neighbor's ill do to you? If he had no ill, he would not even be your enemy. Wish him well, then, that he may end his ill, and he will be your enemy no longer.   AUGUSTINE OF HIPPO

We can never hate another human soul without it at the same time leaving a damaging mark on our own souls.

C. M. M.

The man who truly loves his neighbor, therefore loves also his enemy. . . . We think that it is impossible for a man to love his enemy, alas, for enemies can hardly bear to look at each other. Oh, well, then close our eyes. . .and remember the commandment that thou shalt love, then you love—your enemy? No, then you love your neighbor, for you don't see that he is your enemy.   SOREN KIERKEGAARD

Our life has so diverged from the teaching of Christ that the fiery divergence has become the chief hindrance to our understanding His teaching. We have so disregarded and forgotten all He has said about our way of life—His injunction not merely not to kill, but not even to hate any man; not to defend ourselves but to turn the other cheek and to love our enemies.   LEO TOLSTOY
The Complete Works of Leo Tolstoy

If I would destroy a man, I must cause him to hate me. But I must continue to love him or I will destroy myself. Could a man understand this paradox and still hate?   MARGUERITE HARMON BRO
More Than We Are

Anyone who claims to be in the light but hates his brother is still in the darkness. Whoever loves his brother lives in the light, and there is nothing in him to make him stumble. But whoever hates his brother is in the darkness and walks around in the darkness; he does not know where he is going, because the darkness has blinded him. 1 JOHN 2:9–11

Not only are we to love those who curse us, but we are also to love those who maintain deep seated feelings of hatred toward us. Such hatred will be returned with good deeds. The only Christian way to respond to hate is to heap deeds of kindness upon the one who thus hates us.

A love which limits itself to friends and neighbors is not love at all; it is essentially selfishness.

C. E. COLTON
The Sermon on the Mount

Do not despise others because, as it seems to you, they do not possess the virtues you thought they had: They may be pleasing to God for other reasons which you cannot discover.

JOHN OF THE CROSS
The Living Flame of Love

Closing Prayer

*I pray that you,
being rooted in and established in love,
may have power, together with all the saints,
to grasp how wide and long
and high and deep is the love of Christ,
and to know this love that surpasses knowledge—
that you may be filled to the measure
of all the fullness of God.*

Ephesians 3:17–19

CHAPTER 25

WITH FORGIVENESS COMES PEACE

*Be kind and compassionate to one another,
forgiving each other,
just as in Christ God forgave you.*

EPHESIANS 4:32

Forgiveness, an indispensable prerequisite for coming to the Father, changes bitterness into cheerful cooperation. We must forgive others because God has forgiven us. He commands us to do so. If we are unforgiving, He cannot get into the recesses of our heart where resentments are hidden. Forgiveness clears the way for His love to flow in. How obvious and necessary His command becomes! Forgiving others of wrongs is necessary for our happiness and well-being. We must not only forgive them but wish them every good thing in life and hope that they will become our friends. Forgiveness of enemies and gentle forbearance of wrongs can exert a spiritual influence on others as hate or revenge cannot. To carry a grudge and to live with bitterness is to live in the past. Forgiveness frees a person to live in the present. Let us never under any circumstance retaliate for a wrong done to us. This is not Jesus' way, the way of love, which thinks in terms of doing for others.

Blessed Are the Merciful

We need not climb up into heaven to see whether our sins are forgiven: Let us look into our hearts, and see if we can forgive others. If we can, we need not doubt but God has forgiven us.

Thomas Watson

If I am even with my enemy,
the debt is paid; but if I forgive him,
I oblige him forever.

William Penn
Some Fruits of Solitude

During the Revolutionary War a preacher walked fifty miles to beg General Washington to spare the life of a man who had been sentenced to death for neglect of duty. "I am sorry I cannot grant your request for your friend's pardon," said Washington. The preacher replied: "He is not my friend; I suppose I do not have a worse enemy living." Washington looked surprised and said, "Surely you are not pleading for your enemy?" "Yes!" said the preacher. "Then," said General Washington, "I will grant the pardon." The forgiving spirit of the minister so affected the man that he was transformed from an enemy to a friend.

J. W. BROUGHER

I can forgive, but I cannot forget," is only another way of saying, "I cannot forgive." A forgiveness ought to be like a canceled note, torn in two, and burned up so that it can never be shown against the man.

DWIGHT L. MOODY

Pardon one another so that later on you will not remember the injury. The recollection of an injury is in itself wrong. It adds to our anger, nurtures our sin, and hates what is good. It is a rusty arrow and poison for the soul.

FRANCIS OF PAOLA

Our forgiving of others will not procure forgiveness for ourselves; but our not forgiving others proves that we ourselves are not forgiven.

JOHN OWEN

He drew a circle that shut me out—
Heretic, rebel, a thing to flout,
But love and I had the wit to win:
We drew a circle that took him in.

EDWIN MARKHAM

The best way to destroy your enemy
is to make him your friend.

ABRAHAM LINCOLN

Of him that hopes to be forgiven, it is indispensably required that he forgive. It is therefore superfluous to urge any other motive. On this great duty eternity is suspended; and to him that refuses to practice it, the throne of mercy is inaccessible, and the Savior of the world has been born in vain.

SAMUEL JOHNSON

Do not seek revenge, or bear a grudge against one of your people, but love your neighbor as yourself. I am the LORD" (Leviticus 19:18). How searching is that demand upon the soul! My forgiveness of my brother is to be complete. No sullenness is to remain, no sulky temper which so easily gives birth to thunder and lightning. There is to be no painful aloofness, no assumption of a superiority which rains contempt upon the offender. When I forgive, I am not to carry any powder forward on the journey. I am to empty out all my explosives, all my ammunition of anger and revenge. I am not to "bear any grudge."

I cannot meet this demand. It is altogether beyond me. I might utter words of forgiveness, but I cannot reveal a clear, bright, blue sky without a touch of storm brewing anywhere. But the Lord of grace can do it for me. He can change my weather. He can create a new climate. He can "renew a right spirit within me," and in that holy atmosphere nothing shall live which seeks to poison and destroy. Grudges shall die "like cloud-spots in the dawn." Revenge, that was full reaction of the unclean, feverish soul, shall give place to good-will, the strong genial presence which makes its home in a new heart.

JOHN H. JOWETT
My Daily Meditation

He who has not forgiven an enemy
has not yet tasted one of the
most sublime enjoyments of life.

JOHANN KASPER LAVATER

So when you are presenting your gift at the altar if you remember that your brother has any grievance against you, leave your gift right there before the altar and go make up with your brother and then come back and present your gift." There is something irresistibly logical about the procedure. From a practical point of view it is impossible to give up one's temper and offer one's tongue to God to direct without first making the best possible apology to the person as our tongue has hurt. After that we somehow feel clean before God. Clean and empty and ready for Him to take over just as we asked Him to do.   MARGUERITE HARMON BRO
More Than We Are

He who cannot forgive others breaks the bridge
over which he must pass himself.

GEORGE HERBERT

And when you stand praying, if you hold anything against anyone, forgive him, so that your
Father in heaven may forgive you your sins."

MARK 11:25–26

The quality of mercy is not strained;
It droppeth as the gentle rain from heaven
Upon the place beneath: it is twice blessed;
It blesseth him that gives, and him that takes.

WILLIAM SHAKESPEARE
"Julius Caesar"

Be noble! And the nobleness that lies
In other men, sleeping, but never dead,
Will rise in majesty to meet thine own.

JAMES RUSSELL LOWELL
"Sonnet IV"

He who wishes to revenge injuries
by reciprocated hatred will live in misery.

BARUCH SPINOZA
Ethics

If religion forbids all instances of revenge, without any exception, it is because all revenge is of the nature of poison; and though we do not take so much as to put an end to life, yet if we take any at all, it corrupts the whole mass of blood, and makes it difficult to be restored to health.   WILLIAM LAW
A Serious Call to a Devout and Holy Life

I now understand the words of Jesus: "Ye have heard that it hath been said, 'An eye for an eye, and a tooth for a tooth'; but I say unto you, Do not resist an evil person. If someone strikes you on the right cheek, turn to him the other also." Jesus' meaning is: You have thought that you were acting in a reasonable manner in defending yourself by violence against evil, in tearing out an eye for an eye, by fighting against evil with criminal tribunals, guardians of the peace, armies; but I say unto you, "Renounce violence; have nothing to do with violence; do harm to no one, not even to your enemy."

LEO TOLSTOY

*Revenge is often like biting a dog
because the dog bit you.*

AUSTIN O'MALLEY

When Leonardo da Vinci was painting his great masterpiece, "The Last Supper," he became quite angry with a friend. He lashed out at him with hot, bitter words. Then he threatened the friend with vengeance. Returning to his canvas, he began to paint the face of Jesus. He found, however, that he was so perturbed and upset that he could not compose himself sufficiently to do the delicate work before him. He went out immediately, sought his hurt friend, and humbly asked forgiveness for the tongue-lashing he had given him. Then he was in possession of that inner calm which enabled him to give the Master's face the tender and delicate expression he knew it had to have. C. M. M.

CLOSING PRAYER

O Lord, our God,
by whose power alone we are enabled
to live together as brothers and sisters;
let Your forgiveness make us ready to forgive
and to be reconciled to those
from whom we are estranged;
through Jesus Christ our Lord.
Amen.

CHAPTER 26

We Find Our Own Life in Losing It in Service to Others

*"Now that I, your Lord and Teacher,
have washed your feet, you also should wash
one another's feet."*

JOHN 13:14

Jesus calls us to be servants. As a servant, we serve all whom God sends our way in humbleness and in compassion. Serving others is necessary because it deflates the ego in us, which exalts us at the expense of others. We find freedom in no longer desiring to be in charge. "He who humbles himself, God exalts; he who exalts himself God humbles; from him who searches for greatness, greatness flies; he who flees from greatness, greatness searches out!" Religion is meant to be acted out. You may talk circles around your fellowman and pray in eloquence and not act a speck of it. The wise one speaks little and does much. Only by doing something for others does fulfillment and meaning in life come to us, almost mysteriously, of itself, as God intended.

BY SERVING OUR NEIGHBOR
WE SERVE GOD

Christ has no body now on earth but yours;
Yours are the only hands with which He can do
His work,
Yours are the only feet with which He can go about
the world,
Yours are the only eyes through which His compassion
Can shine forth upon a troubled world.
Christ has no body now on earth but yours.

TERESA OF AVILA

Serve wholeheartedly, as if you were serving the Lord, not men, because you know that the Lord will reward everyone for whatever good he does, whether he is slave or free.   EPHESIANS 6:7

There is so much to be set right in the world, there are so many to be led and helped and comforted, that we must continually come in contact with such in our daily life. Let us only take care, that, by the glance being turned inward, or strained onward, or lost in vacant reverie, we do not miss our turn of service, and pass by those to whom we might have been sent on an errand straight from God.

ELIZABETH CHARLES

The hands that tend the sick tend Christ; the willing feet that go on errands of love, work for Christ; the words of comfort to the sorrowful and of sympathy to the mourner, are spoken in the name of Christ—Christ comforts the world through His friends. How much have you done for Him? ARTHUR F. WINNINGTON INGRAM

The King will reply,
'I tell you the truth,
whatever you did for one of the least
of these brothers of mine,
you did for me.'"

MATTHEW 25:40

As we travel life's earthly road from Jerusalem to Jericho may we be Good Samaritans to all who need us, cheering, healing, and fortifying them with true neighborliness, vitalizing all the relations of life with an unselfish love, remembering that love is the strongest force in the world.

George W. Truett

*Knowing that helping the poor
is in fact helping the Lord makes it possible
to care for others without conditions,
without reservation and
without need for recognition.*

C. M. M.

There are strange ways of serving God;
You sweep a room or turn a sod,
And suddenly, to your surprise,
You hear the whirr of seraphim,
And find you're under God's own eyes
And building palaces for Him.

Hermann Hagedorn

Every individual will be the happier the more clearly he understands that his vocation consists, not in exacting service from others, but in ministering to others, in giving his life the ransom of many. LEO TOLSTOY

We send out our energies in the service of others and there comes back to us that which becomes the food for our souls. RALPH W. SOCKMAN
Paradoxes of Jesus

Nothing is a good work unless it is done with a good motive; and there is no motive which can be said to be good but the glory of God. He who performs good works with a view to save himself, does not do them from a good motive, because his motive is selfish. He who does them also to gain the esteem of his fellows and for the good of society, has a laudable motive, so far as man is concerned; but it is, after all, an inferior motive. What end had we in view? If for the benefit of our fellow-creatures, then let our fellow-creatures pay us; but that has nought to do with God. CHARLES H. SPURGEON
The New Park Street Pulpit, Vol. 2

Once we give up our slavery to the world, which is a cruel master indeed, to become Christ's bond-slave, we live out our servitude to Him by glad service to others. This volunteer slavery cannot be taken advantage of—we have chosen to surrender everything for love. It is a wholly different thing from forced labor. It is, in fact, the purest joy when it is most unobserved, most unself-conscious, most simple, most freely offered.   ELISABETH ELLIOT
A Lamp for My Feet

The truly devout man does not run about seeking for good works, but he waits until the occasion of doing good presents itself to him. He does what in him lies to ensure success; but he leaves the care of the success to God. He prefers those good works which are obscure and done in secret to those which are brilliant and gain general admiration; but he does not shrink from these latter when they are for the glory of God and the edification of his neighbor.   JEAN-NICOLAS GROU
Manual for Interior Souls

A child's kiss,
Set on thy sighing lips, shall make thee glad;
A poor man served by thee, shall make thee rich;
A sick man helped by thee, shall make thee strong,
Thou shalt be served thyself by every sense
Of service which thou renderest.

Elizabeth Barrett Browning,
from "The Sweetest Lives"

Faith Without Works Is Dead

Not everyone who says to me, 'Lord, Lord,' will enter into the kingdom of heaven, but only he who does the will of my Father who is in heaven."

Matthew 7:21

Faith and works are like
the light of a candle;
they cannot be separated.

Joseph Beaumont

Seeing that good works are the witness of the Holy Ghost, man can never do without them. The aim of man is not outward holiness by works, but life in God, yet this last expresses itself in works of love.

MEISTER ECKHART
Sermons

No man has a right to lead such a life of contemplation as to forget in his own ease the service due to his neighbor; nor has any man a right to be so immersed in active life as to neglect the contemplation of God.

AUGUSTINE OF HIPPO

Whatever our works are—good or evil—we are,
for we are the trees and they the fruits.
They show what each of us is.

AUGUSTINE OF HIPPO

Not to ease and aimless quiet
Doth that inward answer tend,
But to works of love and duty
As our being's end.

JOHN GREENLEAF WHITTIER

Christ was the greatest contemplative that ever lived, yet He was ever at the service of men, and never did His ineffable and perpetual contemplation diminish His activity.

JAN VAN RUYSBROECK
Flowers of a Mystic Garden

Anyone who listens to the word but does not do what it says is like a man who looks at his face in a mirror and, after looking at himself, goes away and immediately forgets what he looks like. But the man who looks intently into the perfect law that gives freedom, and continues to do this, not forgetting what he has heard, but doing it—he will be blessed in what he does. JAMES 1:23–25

What good is it, my brothers, if a man claims to have faith but has no deeds? Can such faith save him? Suppose a brother or sister is without clothes and daily food. If one of you says to him, "Go, I wish you well; keep warm and well fed," but does nothing about his physical needs, what good is it? In the same way, faith by itself, if it is not accompanied by action, is dead. JAMES 2:14–17

A Christian should always remember that the value of his good works is not based on their number and excellence, but on the love of God which prompts him to do these things.

JOHN OF THE CROSS

*As the apple is not
the cause of the apple tree,
but a fruit of it:
Even so good works are not
the cause of our salvation,
but a sign and a fruit of the same.*

DANIEL CAWDRAY

THEREFORE, AS WE HAVE OPPORTUNITY,
LET US DO GOOD TO ALL PEOPLE

Poverty is the load of some, and wealth is the load of others, perhaps the greater load of the two. It may weigh them to perdition. Bear the load of your neighbor's poverty, and let him bear with you the load of your wealth. You lightenest your load by lightening his.

AUGUSTINE OF HIPPO

I don't know what your destiny will be, but one thing I know: The only ones among you who will be truly happy are those who will have sought and found how to serve.   ALBERT SCHWEITZER

We must do more than "stand" the waterspouts which break over us and rage round us. Our task is to bind up the brokenhearted, to be a cup of strength in times of agony, to set men on their feet when the foundations seem to be caving in, and to feed and comfort the little children amidst the wreckage of war and devastation.

RUFUS M. JONES
New Eyes for Invisibles

Receive every one who comes to you, especially with a spiritual purpose, with a kind and cheerful aspect, although he or she may be a beggar, and humble yourself inwardly before everybody, counting yourself lower than he or she, for you are placed by Christ Himself to be the servant of all, and all are His members although like you they bear the wounds of sin.   ALEXANDER YELCHANINOV
Diary

If I can stop one heart from breaking,
I shall not live in vain:
If I can ease one life the aching,
Or cool one pain,
Or help one fainting robin
Unto his nest again,
I shall not live in vain.

EMILY DICKINSON

Learn the lesson that,
if you are to do the work of a prophet,
what you need is not a scepter but a hoe.

BERNARD OF CLAIRVAUX

I helped the old lady do her work, helped her wash
her heavy quilts that had gone two years without
washing, to her despair, because she had not help
with them, and can no longer lift them alone from
the water and get them on the line. She cried when
I left!   MARJORIE KINNAN RAWLINGS

Believing in Christ as Savior is inseparable
from being a Christian to your neighbor.

MARTIN LUTHER

The most obvious lesson in Christ's teaching is that there is no happiness in having and getting anything, but only in giving. It consists in giving, and in serving others. He that would be great amongst you, said Christ, let him serve.

HENRY DRUMMOND
The Greatest Thing in the World

The service we render to others is really the rent we pay for our room on this earth. It is obvious that man is himself a traveler; that the purpose of this world is not "to have and to hold" but "to give and to serve." There can be no other meaning.

WILFRED T. GRENFELL

IT IS WHEN YOU GIVE OF YOURSELF
THAT YOU TRULY GIVE

*Rings and jewels are not gifts,
but apologies for gifts.
The only true gift is a portion of thyself.*

RALPH WALDO EMERSON

You and I have an inexhaustible supply of the things people value most highly—smiles, friendliness, understanding, and appreciation. The more we give away, the more we are enriched.

The greatest gifts we can give to others are not material things but gifts of ourselves. The great gifts are those of love, of inspiration, of kindness, of encouragement, of forgiveness, of ideas and ideals. How many great gifts can we give this day? Each day let's do someone a good turn—one that will either not be discovered or will be discovered only by accident. MARGUERITE HARMON BRO
More Than We Are

I gave a beggar from my little store
Of well earned gold.
He spent the shining ore, and came again and yet
   again
Still cold and hungry as before.
I gave the Christ, and through that Christ of mine
He found himself, a man, supreme, divine!
Fed, clothed and crowned with blessings manifold.
   And now he begs no more.

ELLA WHEELER WILCOX

If you spend yourselves in behalf of the hungry and satisfy the needs of the oppressed, then your light will rise in the darkness, and your night will become like the noonday.   ISAIAH 58:10

CLOSING PRAYER

Teach us, Lord,
To serve Thee as Thou deservest;
To give and not to count the cost;
To fight and not to heed the wounds;
To toil and not to seek for rest;
To labor and not to ask for any reward
Save that of knowing that we do Thy will.

IGNATIUS OF LOYOLA

CHAPTER 27

WE REVEAL TO GOD OUR GRATITUDE AND TO OTHERS GOD'S LOVE BY OUR WORDS AND ACTIONS

*Always be prepared to give an answer
to everyone who asks you to give the reason
for the hope that you have.*

1 PETER 3:15

Let us be grateful in every circumstance because we know that God is leading us in the best possible way and He will show us wondrous and mighty things to be thankful for. When we live with constant gratitude, our lives will become a continual prayer of thanksgiving to the Almighty who gives us everything. Every one of us to whom the world comes alive with the love of God will want others to know about our wonderful discovery. We cannot give God to others, but we can drop clues along the way to point them in the right direction. Each one of us is a unique individual and God uses our talents in different ways to reveal His love to others. Let us make sure we are His instruments for telling the good news in whatever way He directs. Missionary work is evidence of life in a church, which in turn produces more life. When we share our faith we find more strength within. We must give Him away in order to have Him. That is the law of God. What one gives, one has. What one keeps, one loses.

GIVE THANKS IN ALL CIRCUMSTANCES

Thanksgiving has a curative power. The heart that is constantly overflowing with gratitude will be seen from those attacks of resentfulness and gloom that bother so many religious persons. A thankful heart cannot be cynical!

A. W. TOZER
Renewed Day by Day

We are to thank God in all things; the Lord knows what is best for us, and He is ordering the course of our life, bringing the details to pass in the time and manner of His desire. He has never made a mistake, and what He allows to come into the life of His child is for the good of that child and for our profit. DONALD GREY BARNHOUSE
Illustrating Great Themes of Scripture

I shall try to remember all this day that I am a divine creation with infinite possibilities.

BENJAMIN EITELGEORGE

Flowers rejoice when night is done,
Lift their heads to greet the sun;
Sweetest looks and odors raise,
In a silent hymn of praise.

So my heart would turn away
From the darkness to the day;
Lying open in God's sight
Like a flower in the light.

HENRY VAN DYKE

Enter his gates with thanksgiving
and his courts with praise;
give thanks to him and praise his name.
*For the L*ORD *is good and his love endures forever;*
his faithfulness continues through all generations.

PSALM 100:4–5

When we humble ourselves and realize that we are not the center of the world and that all things do not revolve around us, but around God, we are grateful to be the stewards of whatever wealth we possess. In addition to providing for our physical needs, He has provided for our spiritual and emotional needs through the wonder and joy of nature, of family, of miracles and gifts abounding all around us. When we see all His goodness to us we are filled with gratitude and thanksgiving.   C. M. M.

Learn the lesson of Thanksgiving. It is due to God, it is due to ourselves. Thanksgiving for the past makes us trustful in the present and hopeful for the future. What He has done is the pledge of what He will do.   ARTHUR C. A. HALL

There were ten lepers healed, and only one turned back to give thanks, but it is to be noticed that our Lord did not recall His gift from the other nine because of their lack of gratitude. When we begin to lessen our acts of kindness and helpfulness because we think those who receive do not properly appreciate what is done for them, it is time to question our own motives. AUTHOR UNKNOWN

This is the day the LORD has made;
let us rejoice and be glad in it.

PSALM 118:24

He is a wise man who does not grieve for the things which he has not, but rejoices for those which he has. EPICTETUS
Discourses

Let never day nor night unhallow'd pass,
But still remember what the Lord hath done.

WILLIAM SHAKESPEARE

God, we thank You for this earth, our homes; for the wide sky and the blessed sun, for the salt sea and the running water, for the everlasting hills and the never resting winds, for trees and the common grass underfoot. We thank You for our senses by which we hear the songs of birds, and see the splendor of the summer fields, and taste of the autumn fruits, and rejoice in the feel of the snow, and smell the breath of the spring. Grant us a heart wide open to all this beauty; and save our souls from being so blind that we pass unseeing when even the common thorn bush is aflame with Your glory, O God our creator, who lives and reigns for ever and ever.

WALTER RAUSCHENBUSCH

It is certain that whatever seeming calamity happens to you, if you thank and praise God for it, you turn it into a blessing. Could you therefore work miracles, you could not do more for yourself, than by this thankful spirit, for it heals with a word speaking, and turns all that it touches into happiness.   WILLIAM LAW

WE ARE CHRIST'S AMBASSADORS

We will win the world when we realize that fellowship, not evangelism, must be our primary emphasis. When we demonstrate the big Miracle of Love, it won't be necessary for us to go out—they will come in. . . . People don't go where the action is, they go where love is.   JESS MOODY

Go and make disciples of all nations,
baptizing them in the name of the
Father and of the Son and of the Holy Spirit,
and teaching them to obey everything
I have commanded you."

MATTHEW 28:19–20

*The joy of finding the everywhereness of God
cannot be presented to someone else
like a gift on a platter but only as a clue.*

MARGUERITE HARMON BRO
More Than We Are

*There are two ways of spreading light:
to be the candle or the mirror that reflects it.*

EDITH WHARTON

If Christ lives in us,
controlling our personalities,
we will leave glorious marks
on the lives we touch.
Not because of our lovely characters,
but because of His.

EUGENIA PRICE

The most important part of our task is to tell everyone who will listen that Jesus is the only answer to the problems that are disturbing the hearts of men and nations. We shall have the right to speak because we can tell from experience that His light is more powerful than the deepest darkness. . . . How wonderful that the reality of His presence is greater than the reality of the hell about us.   BETSIE TEN BOOM,
to her sister, CORRIE,
both in a concentration camp

This is the key. We have come into this spiritual experience. We find it in ourselves sometimes by fire or earthquake, but more often by a still small voice. It changes our way of thinking, our way of dealing with our fellowman. We then seek to share it with others whose divine seed needs to be nourished so it will germinate. We see this need and having been given orders from the Lord Himself, we set out to go wherever there is a need and to share this life changing discovery.   C. M. M.

For what are the servants of the Lord
but His minstrels who
should raise the hearts of men
and move them to spiritual joy.

FRANCIS OF ASSISI

The secret of religion isn't well-known. It's the secret of living. Only a few have found it, and they can't pass it on. They can only inspire others to keep searching. They can only plant the seed and hope the soil is right.   ANONYMOUS

Journal of an Ordinary Pilgrim

Kindness has converted more sinners than zeal, eloquence, or learning. Kind words are the music of the world. They have a power which seems to be beyond natural causes, as if they were some angel's song which had lost its way and come on earth. It seems as if they could almost do what in reality God alone can do—soften the hard and angry hearts of men. No one was ever corrected by a sarcasm—crushed, perhaps, if the sarcasm was clever enough, but drawn nearer to God, never.

FREDERICK W. FABER

Those who are wise will shine like
the brightness of the heavens,
and those who lead many to righteousness,
like the stars for ever and ever."

DANIEL 12:3

One who can be positively depended upon, who is faithful in the least things as well as in the greatest, whose life and character are true through and through, gives out a light in this world which honors Christ and blesses others.

JAMES R. MILLER

You perhaps may ask why I go on writing books myself if there is but one teacher: Answer, though there is but one bridegroom that can furnish the blessing of the marriage feast, yet His servants are sent out to invite the guests. This is the unalterable difference between Christ's teaching and the teaching of those who only publish the glad tidings of Him. They are not the bridegroom and therefore have not the bridegroom's voice. They are not the light, but only sent to bear witness of it. And as the Baptist said, "He must increase, but I must decrease"; so every faithful teacher saith of his doctrine, it must decrease and end as soon as it has led to the true Teacher.   WILLIAM LAW
A Collection of Letters

You are the light of the world. A city on a hill cannot be hidden. Neither do people light a lamp and put it under a bowl. Instead they put it on its stand, and it gives light to everyone in the house. In the same way, let your light shine before men, that they may see your good deeds and praise your Father in heaven."   MATTHEW 5:14–16

Don't let us think that we need to be "stars" in order to shine. It was by the ministry of a candle that the woman recovered her lost piece of silver.

JOHN HENRY JOWETT

CLOSING PRAYER

Dear Lord,
help me to spread Your fragrance everywhere
I go—let me preach You without preaching,
not by words but by my example—
by the catching force,
the sympathetic influence of what I do,
the evident fullness of the love
my heart bears to You.
Amen.

JOHN H. NEWMAN

AUTHOR INDEX

CREDITS

Barbour Publishing, Inc., expresses its appreciation to all those who generously gave permission to reprint and/or adapt copyrighted material. Diligent effort has been made to identify, locate, and contact copyright holders, and to secure permission to use copyrighted material. If any permissions or acknowledgments have been inadvertently omitted or if such permissions were not received by the time of publication, the publisher would sincerely appreciate receiving complete information so that correct credit can be given in future editions.

Inspirational Library

Beautiful purse/pocket-size editions of Christian classics bound in flexible leatherette. These books make thoughtful gifts for everyone on your list, including yourself!

When I'm on My Knees   The highly popular collection of devotional thoughts on prayer, especially for women.
    Flexible Leatherette. $4.97

The Bible Promise Book   Over 1,000 promises from God's Word arranged by topic. What does God promise about matters like: Anger, Illness, Jealousy, Love, Money, Old Age, and Mercy? Find out in this book!
    Flexible Leatherette. $3.97

Daily Wisdom for Women   A daily devotional for women seeking biblical wisdom to apply to their lives. Scripture taken from the New American Standard Version of the Bible.
    Flexible Leatherette. $4.97

My Daily Prayer Journal   Each page is dated and features a Scripture verse and ample room for you to record your thoughts, prayers, and praises. One page for each day of the year.
    Flexible Leatherette. $4.97

Available wherever books are sold.
Or order from:

Barbour Publishing, Inc.
P.O. Box 719
Uhrichsville, OH 44683
http://www.barbourbooks.com

If you order by mail, add $2.00 to your order for shipping.
Prices are subject to change without notice.